Baking

Bounty Books

Introduction

With the right recipe, plus a pinch of patience, a dash of common sense, and a sprinkling of attention to detail, we can all bake the perfect cake! So prepare to fill your kitchen with the mouth-watering aroma of home-baked treats, as you turn out truly scrumptious cakes, cookies and desserts. Family and friends will love you for it!

This paperback edition published in 2011 by Bounty Books,
a division of Octopus Publishing Group Limited,
Endeavour House, 189 Shaftesbury Avenue, London WC2H 8JY
www.octopusbooks.co.uk

An Hachette UK Company
www.hachette.co.uk

Reprinted 2011, 2012

ISBN: 978-0-753722-08-4

Printed and bound in China

contents

tips & techniques

Baking a perfect cake may not be rocket science – but it does require a little background knowledge and a lot of attention to detail. The tips on the following pages will help set you straight.

Greasing tin with brush and melted butter

oven types and rack position

There are many different types of ovens and energy sources, so it is important that you get to know your oven – particularly when it comes to baking cakes. The recipes in this book were tested in domestic-size electric ovens.

- If using a fan-assisted oven, check the operating instructions for best results. As a rule, reduce the baking temperature by 10°C to 20°C when using the fan during baking; cakes might also take slightly less time to bake than specified. Some ovens give better results if the fan is used for part of the baking time; it is usually best to introduce the fan about halfway through the baking time.
- None of the recipes in this book has been tested in a microwave or microwave/convection oven, as the baking time and result would be different from a conventionally baked cake.
- We positioned the oven racks and cake tin(s) so that the top of the baked cake will be roughly in the centre of the oven. If in doubt, check the manufacturer's instructions for your oven.
- Several cakes can be baked at the same time, either on the same or different racks, provided they do not touch each other, or the oven wall or door, to allow for even circulation of heat.
- To ensure even browning, cake tins on different racks should exchange positions about halfway through baking time; move the lower cakes to the top rack, and vice versa. This will not affect results if you do this carefully and quickly.
- Best results are obtained by baking cakes in an oven preheated to the desired temperature; this takes about 10 minutes. This rule is particularly important for cakes which bake in under 30 minutes.
- For oven temperatures, see page 96.

Sprinkling flour over greased area

Tracing around the base of tin

how to prepare a cake tin

To grease a cake tin, use either a light, even coating of cooking-oil spray, or a pastry brush to brush melted butter or margarine evenly over the base and side(s).

Sometimes recipes call for a greased and floured cake tin. Simply grease the tin evenly (melted butter is best in this case) and allow it to 'set' a minute or two before sprinkling a little flour evenly over the greased area. Tap the tin several times on your work surface then tip out the excess flour.

Cakes that are high in sugar, or that contain golden syrup, treacle or honey, have a tendency to stick so we recommend lining the base and/or side(s) of the pans. We have indicated in the recipes when this is necessary.

Trace around the base of the pan with a pencil onto greaseproof paper or baking; parchment; cut out the shape, slightly inside the pencil mark, so the paper fits snugly inside the greased pan. It is not necessary to grease the baking parchment once it is in position.

Placing baking-parchment collar in tin

As a guide, cakes requiring 1 hour or longer to bake should have a baking parchment 'collar', extending about 5cm (2in) above the edge of the tin, to protect the top of the cake. The following method of lining round or square cake tins allows for this, using greaseproof or baking parchment:

- For side(s), cut three paper strips long enough to fit around inside of the tin and 8cm (3¼in) wider than the depth of the tin. Fold strips lengthways about 2cm (¾in) from the edge and make short diagonal cuts about 2cm (¾in) apart, up to the fold. This helps ease the paper around the curves or corners of the tin, with cut section fitting around the base.
- Using base of tin as a guide, cut three paper circles (or squares) as instructed previously; position in base of tin after lining sides.

CAKE TINS

- We used aluminium cake tins throughout this book as they give the best cake-baking results.
- Cake tins made from materials having various coatings, such as non-stick, work well provided that the surface is unscratched. Pans made from tin and stainless steel do not conduct heat as evenly as does aluminium.
- We found that oven temperatures should be lowered slightly (by about 10°C) when using cake tins other than those made of aluminium.

cooking, cooling & keeping

to test if a cake is cooked

All cake baking times are approximate. Check your cake just after the suggested cooking time; it should have become browned and have started to shrink from the side(s) of the tin. Feel the top gently with your fingertips; it should feel firm.

You may want to insert a thin skewer in the deepest part of the cake from top to base (we prefer to use a metal skewer rather than a wooden one because any mixture that adheres to it is easier to see). Gently remove the skewer; it shouldn't have any uncooked cake mixture clinging to it (see picture). Do not confuse the appearance of the cake mixture with stickiness from fruit.

CAKE MAKING TIPS

- We do not recommend mixing cakes in blenders or food processors unless specified in the particular recipe concerned.
- Use an electric beater to mix cakes, and always have the ingredients at room temperature, particularly the butter. Melted or extremely soft butter will alter the texture of the baked cake.
- Start mixing ingredients on a low speed; once mixture is combined, increase the speed to about medium and beat for the required time.
- Creamed mixtures for cakes can be mixed with a wooden spoon, but this takes longer.
- When measuring liquids, always stand the marked measuring jug on a flat surface and check at eye level for accuracy.
- Spoon measurements should be levelled off with a knife or spatula. Be careful when measuring ingredients such as honey or treacle.

cooling a cake

We have suggested standing cakes for up to 30 minutes before turning onto wire racks to cool further. The best way to do this, after standing time has elapsed, is to hold the cake tin firmly and shake it gently, thus loosening the cake from the tin. Turn the cake, upside down, onto a wire rack, then turn the cake top-side up immediately using a second rack (see picture). Some wire racks mark the cakes, particularly soft cakes such as sponges. To prevent this, cover the rack with baking parchment.

We have indicated when it is best to cool cakes in tins; these are always covered with foil before cooling, and are mostly fruit cakes.

HOW TO KEEP A CAKE

We have suggested maximum cake-keeping times at the end of each recipe. Most cakes keep well for 2 or 3 days depending on the climate and type of cake but, as a rule, remember that the higher the fat content, the longer the cake keeps.

- Make sure your cake is at room temperature before storing it in an airtight container as close in size to the cake as possible; this minimises the amount of air around the cake.
- For those cakes that are well suited to freezing, it is usually better to freeze them unfilled and un-iced because icing often cracks during the thawing process. Cakes thaw best overnight in the refrigerator. Wrap or seal cakes in freezer wrap or freezer bags, expelling as much air as possible.
- We prefer to store rich fruit cakes in the refrigerator simply because they'll cut better; once sliced, they quickly return to room temperature.

what went wrong?

Unfortunately, cakes don't always emerge from the oven looking just like our photographs. The following is a troubleshooters' guide to get you and your cake(s) back on track.

my butter cake wasn't perfect...

SINKS IN CENTRE WHILE STILL BAKING If the mixture is forced to rise too quickly because the oven is too hot, it will sink in the centre.
SINKS IN CENTRE AFTER REMOVAL FROM OVEN This generally means that the cake is undercooked.
SUGARY CRUST Butter and sugar have not been creamed sufficiently.
WHITE SPECKS ON TOP Undissolved sugar, or insufficient creaming. In a light butter cake, it is better to use caster sugar, which dissolves easily.

EXCESSIVE SHRINKING The oven being too hot has caused cake to overcook.
RISES AND CRACKS IN CENTRE Cake tin too small or oven too hot. Most cakes baked in loaf, bar or ring tins crack slightly due to the confined space.
CRUMBLES WHEN CUT Mixture may have been creamed too much, or eggs added too quickly, causing curdling.
STICKS TO TIN Too much sugar or other sweetening in recipe. If a recipe contains honey or golden syrup, or if you're using a new tin, it is wise to line the evenly greased pan with greased baking parchment.
COLLAR AROUND TOP OUTSIDE EDGE Cake baked at too high a temperature.
PALE ON TOP, BROWN UNDERNEATH AND SIDES Too large a tin, or lining paper too high around sides of tin.
COLOUR STREAKS ON TOP Insufficient mixing of ingredients, or bowl scrapings not mixed thoroughly into cake mixture in tin.
UNEVEN RISING Oven shelf not straight, stove not level on floor, or mixture not spread evenly in tin.
HOLES IN BAKED CAKE Mixture not creamed sufficiently or oven too hot.
CRUSTY, OVERBROWNED, UNCOOKED IN CENTRE Cake baked too long or at too high a temperature. Cake tin too small, causing top to overcook while cake not cooked through completely.

my rich fruit cake wasn't perfect...

FRUIT SINKS TO BOTTOM Fruit washed but not dried thoroughly; cake mixture too soft to support weight of fruit (caused by over-creaming). Self-raising flour may have been used in recipe instead of plain flour. Fruit should be finely chopped so mixture can support it more easily.

CREAMED MIXTURE CURDLES Eggs and butter not at room temperature to begin with, or eggs not added quickly enough to creamed butter and sugar mixture, or eggs used are too large for mixture to absorb the excess liquid. If eggs used are larger than 60g in weight, omit one of the number shown in ingredients list, or add only the yolk of one of the eggs. Curdled creamed mixture could cause the finished cake to crumble when cut.
DOUGHY IN CENTRE Cake baked in too cold an oven, or not long enough.
BURNT BOTTOM Wrong oven position. Cake baked at too high a temperature, or incorrect lining of tins. Rich fruit cakes require protection during long, slow baking time. Cakes which are 22cm (9in) or smaller require three thicknesses of baking-parchment lining; larger cakes need one or two sheets of brown paper and three sheets of baking parchment.
CRACKS ON TOP Cake baked at too high a temperature.
SINKS IN MIDDLE Self-raising flour used, or too much bicarbonate of soda. (Usually only plain flour is used in rich fruit cake, but sometimes a small portion of self-raising flour is added). Cake may not have been baked properly. To test, push sharp-pointed knife through centre to base of tin; blade surface helps distinguish between uncooked mixture or fruit and cooked mixture. Test only after minimum specified baking time.
CRUSTY TOP Cake may have been baked at too high a temperature, on wrong shelf of oven, or too long. Cake should be baked in lower half of oven, at a slow temperature. If cake is 25cm (10in) or over, oven should be reduced to very slow after 1 hour of baking time. Lining paper should extend 5–7cm (2–3in) above edge of tin; if it doesn't, the cake mixture will not be sufficiently protected during the long baking time. A crusty top will also occur if cake is not cooled correctly. When cake is removed from oven, brush top evenly with sherry, rum or brandy. Wrap cake, still in its tin, in aluminium foil to keep it airtight; this traps steam and helps keep top soft.
COLOUR STREAKS ON TOP Insufficient mixing of ingredients, or bowl scrapings not mixed thoroughly into cake mixture in tin.
UNEVEN ON TOP Oven shelf or stove not level, or mixture not spread evenly in tin (use a wet spatula to level top of cake mixture).

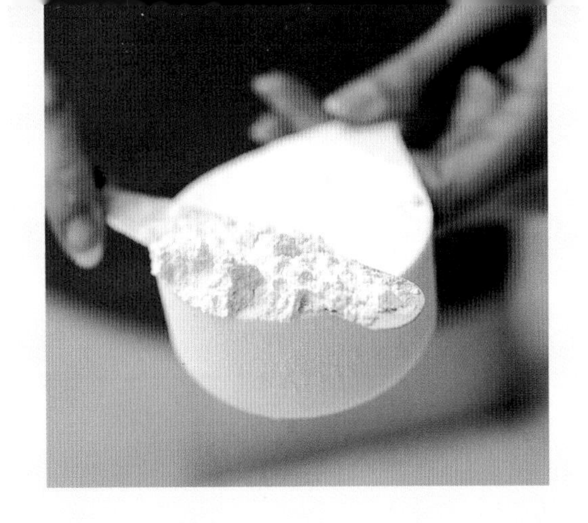

HOW TO MEASURE

- Level top of measuring spoons with a knife.
- When measuring liquids, place a clear glass or plastic jug with metric markings on a flat surface to check accuracy at eye level.
- For conversion charts, see page 96.

my sponge cake wasn't perfect...

SHRINKS IN OVEN Cake baked at too high a temperature or for too long.
SHRINKS AND WRINKLES DURING COOLING Insufficient baking time, or cooling the cake in a draught.
SMALL WHITE SPECKS ON TOP Undissolved sugar; sugar should be added gradually to beaten eggs and beaten until completely dissolved between additions.
FLAT AND TOUGH Incorrect folding in of the flour and liquid. Triple-sifted flour should be folded into mixture in a gentle, circular motion.
PALE AND STICKY ON TOP Baking at too low an oven temperature, or wrong oven position.
CRUSTY Baking at too high an oven temperature, wrong oven position, or tin too small. Using high-sided cake tins protects the cake mixture.
STREAKS ON TOP Scrapings from mixing bowl not mixed into sponge mixture; scrapings are always slightly darker than the full amount of mixture.
SINKS IN CENTRE Tin too small, causing cake to rise quickly, then fall in the centre. Oven temperature may be too high, also causing sponge to rise too quickly. Sponge may be undercooked or oven door may have been opened during first half of baking.

tea cakes to cut

carrot cake with lemon cream cheese frosting

PREPARATION TIME 35 MINUTES BAKING TIME 1 HOUR 15 MINUTES

250ml VEGETABLE OIL
250g FIRMLY PACKED BROWN SUGAR
3 EGGS
3 LARGE CARROTS (540g), COARSELY GRATED
120g COARSELY CHOPPED WALNUTS
375g SELF-RAISING FLOUR
½ TEASPOON BICARBONATE OF SODA
2 TEASPOONS MIXED SPICE

LEMON CREAM CHEESE FROSTING
30g BUTTER, SOFTENED
80g CREAM CHEESE, SOFTENED
1 TEASPOON FINELY GRATED LEMON RIND
240g ICING SUGAR

1 Position oven shelves; preheat oven to moderate. Grease deep 22cm (9in) round cake tin, line base with baking parchment.
2 Beat oil, sugar and eggs in small bowl with electric mixer until thick and creamy.
3 Transfer mixture to large bowl; using wooden spoon, stir in carrot and nuts then sifted dry ingredients. Pour mixture into prepared tin.
4 Bake cake in moderate oven about 1¼ hours. Stand cake 5 minutes then turn onto wire rack; turn cake top-side up to cool.
5 Spread cold cake with lemon cream cheese frosting.

LEMON CREAM CHEESE FROSTING Beat butter, cream cheese and rind in small bowl with electric mixer until light and fluffy; gradually beat in icing sugar.

SERVES 12

TIPS Cover cake loosely with foil during baking if it starts to overbrown.
- Use a light blended vegetable oil, such as corn, safflower or rapeseed oil.
- Use commercially made cream cheese, such as full-fat Philadelphia.
- Pecans can be substituted for walnuts.

STORAGE Cake will keep up to 3 days if refrigerated in an airtight container. Frosted or unfrosted, the cake can be frozen for up to 3 months.

TIPS For best results, use butter, milk and eggs that have reached room temperature. There is no need to sift the dry ingredients; however, if the bicarbonate of soda is lumpy, push it through a small sieve.

Any essence can be substituted for vanilla; for a citrus flavour, add 2 teaspoons finely grated rind, such as orange, lemon or lime.

To give this cake a slight caramel flavour, substitute 275g firmly packed brown sugar for the caster sugar.

STORAGE This cake will keep in an airtight container for up to 3 days. Butter cake can be frozen for up to 3 months.

cut 'n' keep butter cake

PREPARATION TIME 15 MINUTES BAKING TIME 1 HOUR 15 MINUTES

125g BUTTER, SOFTENED
1 TEASPOON VANILLA ESSENCE
275g CASTER SUGAR
3 EGGS
150g PLAIN FLOUR
75g SELF-RAISING FLOUR
¼ TEASPOON BICARBONATE OF SODA
125ml MILK

1 Position oven shelves; preheat oven to moderately low. Grease deep 20cm (8in) round cake tin; line base with baking parchment.
2 Beat ingredients in medium bowl on low speed with electric mixer until just combined.
3 Beat on medium speed until mixture is smooth and changed to a paler colour. Pour mixture into prepared tin.
4 Bake cake in moderately low oven about 1¼ hours. Stand cake 5 minutes then turn onto wire rack; turn cake top-side up to cool. Dust cake with a little sifted icing sugar, if desired.

SERVES 22

This is an easy-to-mix, one-bowl, plain cake – and there's nothing nicer with a cuppa. Simply dust it with a little sifted icing sugar when serving.

almond butter cake

PREPARATION TIME 20 MINUTES BAKING TIME 1 HOUR

375g BUTTER, SOFTENED
1 TEASPOON ALMOND ESSENCE
330g CASTER SUGAR
6 EGGS
110g SELF-RAISING FLOUR
225g PLAIN FLOUR
60g GROUND ALMONDS

1 Position oven shelves; preheat oven to moderate. Grease deep 23cm (9in) square cake tin; line base with baking parchment.
2 Beat butter, essence and sugar in large bowl with electric mixer until light and fluffy; beat in eggs, one at a time, until combined between additions.
3 Using wooden spoon, stir in flours and ground almonds, in two batches. Spread mixture into prepared tin.
4 Bake cake in moderate oven about 1 hour. Stand cake 5 minutes then turn onto wire rack; turn top-side up to cool. Dust cake with a little sifted icing sugar, if desired.

SERVES 16

A yummy, buttery cake best indulged in by grown-ups, as most children don't like the almond flavour.

TIPS Try substituting ground hazelnuts for the almonds, and use vanilla instead of almond essence.
■ This is one of those cakes that must be aerated well to achieve its light, ethereal texture, so be certain to beat the butter, essence, sugar and eggs well.

STORAGE Cake will keep well in an airtight container for up to 3 days at room temperature or up to 1 week in an airtight container in the refrigerator. Cake can be frozen for up to 3 months.

best-ever sponge cake

PREPARATION TIME 25 MINUTES BAKING TIME 25 MINUTES

4 EGGS
165g CASTER SUGAR
150g SELF-RAISING FLOUR
1 TABLESPOON CORNFLOUR
10g BUTTER
80ml BOILING WATER
110g LEMON BUTTER
180ml WHIPPING CREAM
1 TABLESPOON ICING SUGAR

With just a little practice, anyone can become an expert sponge-maker. Read our tips below to help you on your way.

1 Position oven shelves; preheat oven to moderate. Grease two deep 20cm (8in) round cake tins.
2 Beat eggs in large bowl with electric mixer until thick and foamy. Gradually add sugar, about a tablespoonful at a time, beating until sugar is dissolved between additions. Total beating time should be about 10 minutes.
3 Sift flour and cornflour together three times onto paper.
4 Sift flour mixture over egg mixture; using one hand like a rake, quickly and lightly fold and pull flour mixture through egg mixture, using the side of your hand as a scraper to make sure all the ingredients are combined.
5 Pour combined butter and the water down side of bowl; using one hand, fold through egg mixture. Pour mixture evenly into prepared tins, using metal spatula, spread mixture to edges of tins.
6 Bake sponges in moderate oven about 25 minutes. Immediately sponges are baked, turn onto wire racks covered with baking parchment; turn top-side up to cool.
7 Place one sponge on serving plate, spread with lemon butter and whipped cream. Top with remaining cake, dust with sifted icing sugar.

SERVES 8

TIPS Beating the eggs and sugar well helps to correctly aerate the mixture. Caster sugar dissolves the fastest; crystal sugar can be used, but it requires longer beating to be incorporated.
■ If you don't like using your hand to mix ingredients, use a rubber or plastic spatula, or a large metal spoon.
■ It is important to create volume in the egg and sugar mixture; if you don't have a bowl like the one pictured, use a small bowl with deep sides and beat the mixture with either a hand-held or stand-mixer. You will get better results this way, even though you have to transfer the sponge mixture to a larger bowl to fold in the flour and water.
■ When the sponge is cooked, it will feel springy when touched gently with fingertips, and will have shrunk slightly away from the side of tin.
■ Turn the sponge from cake tin as soon as it is baked, or heat from the tin will continue to cook it, giving it a too-crisp crust.

STORAGE Sponge is best made on day of serving. Refrigerate if it is to be filled more than an hour ahead. Unfilled sponge can be frozen for up to 1 month.

Fourth sifting of flour over egg mixture

Folding flour through egg mixture

Folding butter and water through egg mixture

cinnamon tea cake

PREPARATION TIME 15 MINUTES BAKING TIME 30 MINUTES

60g BUTTER, SOFTENED
1 TEASPOON VANILLA ESSENCE
150g CASTER SUGAR
1 EGG
150g SELF-RAISING FLOUR
80ml MILK
10g BUTTER, MELTED, EXTRA
1 TEASPOON GROUND CINNAMON
1 TABLESPOON CASTER SUGAR, EXTRA

1 Position oven shelves; preheat oven to moderate. Grease deep 20cm (8in) round cake tin; line base with baking parchment.
2 Beat butter, essence, sugar and egg in small bowl with electric mixer until very light and fluffy; this process will take between 5 and 10 minutes, depending on the type of mixer used.
3 Using wooden spoon, gently stir in sifted flour and milk. Spread mixture into prepared tin.
4 Bake cake in moderate oven about 30 minutes. Turn cake onto wire rack then turn top-side up; brush top with extra butter, sprinkle with combined cinnamon and extra sugar. Serve warm with butter, if desired.

SERVES 10

Taking care to thoroughly beat the butter, essence, sugar and egg will result in a light-as-air texture to this cake, best when eaten warm with butter.

TIPS The beauty of this cake is its lightness; most of the time in baking it is not necessary to sift flour, but this cake benefits from aeration, and sifting the flour will help lighten the mixture.
■ To change the cake's flavour, omit the vanilla and substitute the essence of your choice, or beat in 2 teaspoons finely grated citrus rind (orange, lemon, lime, mandarin, etc) with the butter mixture.
■ Melt the extra butter in a microwave oven on HIGH (100%) for 10 seconds.

STORAGE This cake should be eaten immediately it is made.

TIPS Any kind of nut can be substituted for the walnuts. Buy exactly the same weight of either ready-ground nuts or of nut pieces that you can blend or process yourself. Pecans and orange, instead of lemon, is another good combination.

- Rum is a good substitute for the brandy, or you can use fruit juice if you don't want to use alcohol.
- Serve this cake warm, or at room temperature, with a little yogurt.

STORAGE Cake with syrup can be kept in an airtight container for up to 2 days. Cake without syrup can be kept in an airtight container for up to 2 days, and can be frozen for up to 3 months.

brandied walnut cake with lemon syrup

PREPARATION TIME 20 MINUTES BAKING TIME 1 HOUR

200g WALNUTS, TOASTED
125g BUTTER, SOFTENED
3 TEASPOONS FINELY GRATED LEMON RIND
150g CASTER SUGAR
1 EGG
2 TABLESPOONS BRANDY
50g PLAIN FLOUR
50g SELF-RAISING FLOUR

LEMON SYRUP
60ml LEMON JUICE
55g CASTER SUGAR

1 Position oven shelves; preheat oven to moderately low. Grease deep 20cm (8in) round cake tin; line base with baking parchment.
2 Blend or process nuts until finely ground.
3 Beat butter, rind, sugar and egg in small bowl with electric mixer until light and fluffy. Transfer mixture to large bowl; using wooden spoon, stir in brandy, nuts and flours. Spread mixture into prepared tin.
4 Bake cake in moderately low oven about 1 hour.
5 Pour hot lemon syrup over hot cake in tin. Cover tin tightly with foil; cool cake to room temperature.

LEMON SYRUP Combine ingredients in small saucepan. Using wooden spoon, stir over heat, without boiling, until sugar dissolves; bring to a boil, remove from heat.

SERVES 12

The walnuts, ground very finely, make up the majority of the 'flour' content of this mixture.

hummingbird cake

PREPARATION TIME 35 MINUTES BAKING TIME 40 MINUTES

This moist, luscious cake from the American Deep South translates as delicious in anyone's language.

It is really important to drain the canned pineapple thoroughly in this recipe. If you don't the cake will be soggy. Cream cheese frosting is a favourite, but, if you prefer, top the cake with a simple icing made using some of the pineapple syrup. Sift 320g icing sugar into a bowl, stir in 2 teaspoons vegetable oil then about 2 tablespoons pineapple syrup. The mixture should be pasty in texture. When the cake is turned out of the pan to cool, spread the icing onto the hot cake. It will set when the cake is cold.

450g CAN CRUSHED PINEAPPLE IN SYRUP
150g PLAIN FLOUR
75g SELF-RAISING FLOUR
½ TEASPOON BICARBONATE OF SODA
½ TEASPOON GROUND CINNAMON
½ TEASPOON GROUND GINGER
200g FIRMLY PACKED BROWN SUGAR
45g DESICCATED COCONUT
2 LARGE OVERRIPE (460g) BANANAS, MASHED
2 EGGS, BEATEN LIGHTLY
180ml VEGETABLE OIL

CREAM CHEESE FROSTING
30g BUTTER, SOFTENED
60g CREAM CHEESE, SOFTENED
1 TEASPOON VANILLA ESSENCE
240g ICING SUGAR

1 Position oven shelves; preheat oven to moderate. Grease deep 23cm (9in) square cake tin, line base with baking parchment.
2 Drain pineapple over medium bowl, pressing with spoon to extract as much syrup as possible. Reserve 60ml syrup.
3 Sift flours, soda, spices and sugar into large bowl. Using wooden spoon, stir in drained pineapple, reserved syrup, coconut, banana, egg and oil; pour into prepared tin.
4 Bake cake in moderate oven about 40 minutes. Stand cake 5 minutes then turn onto wire rack; turn cake top-side up to cool.
5 Spread cold cake with cream cheese frosting.

CREAM CHEESE FROSTING Beat butter, cream cheese and essence in small bowl with electric mixer until light and fluffy; gradually beat in icing sugar.

SERVES 12

STORAGE Cake will keep for up to 3 days in an airtight container in the refrigerator. Frosted or unfrosted, the cake can be frozen for up to 3 months.

TIPS Use a light blended vegetable oil, such as corn, safflower or rapeseed oil.

Drain the pineapple well; too much syrup will result in a heavy cake. Canned crushed pineapple gives better results than blended or processed fresh or canned pieces or slices.

The bananas must be overripe: the fruit's natural starch is converted to sugar during ripening, and it's this natural sugar that contributes to the correct balance of ingredients.

Overripe bananas freeze well. Place overripe fruit straight into your freezer: the skin will blacken, but the fruit inside is fine to use.

Use commercially made cream cheese, such as full-fat Philadelphia.

Toasted shredded coconut is delicious sprinkled over the frosting.

banana cake with passionfruit icing

PREPARATION TIME 35 MINUTES BAKING TIME 50 MINUTES

125g BUTTER, SOFTENED
150g FIRMLY PACKED BROWN SUGAR
2 EGGS
225g SELF-RAISING FLOUR
½ TEASPOON BICARBONATE OF SODA
1 TEASPOON MIXED SPICE
2 LARGE OVERRIPE BANANAS (460g), MASHED
120ml SOURED CREAM
60ml MILK

PASSIONFRUIT ICING
240g ICING SUGAR
1 TEASPOON SOFT BUTTER
2 TABLESPOONS PASSIONFRUIT PULP, APPROXIMATELY

1 Position oven shelves; preheat oven to moderate. Grease 15cm x 25cm (6in x 10in) loaf tin; line base with baking parchment.
2 Beat butter and sugar in small bowl with electric mixer until light and fluffy. Beat in eggs, one at a time, until combined. Transfer mixture to large bowl; using wooden spoon, stir in sifted dry ingredients, banana, cream and milk. Spread mixture into prepared tin.
3 Bake cake in moderate oven about 50 minutes. Stand cake 5 minutes then turn onto wire rack; turn cake top-side up to cool.
4 Spread cold cake with passionfruit icing.

PASSIONFRUIT ICING Place icing sugar in small heatproof bowl, stir in butter and enough pulp to give a firm paste. Stir over hot water until icing is of spreading consistency, taking care not to overheat; use immediately.

SERVES 10

TIPS It is important that the bananas you use are overripe: not only do they mash easily but, if they are underripe, the cake will be too heavy.
■ The icing must be made in a heatproof bowl, preferably one made from glass or china. Stand the bowl over a saucepan of barely simmering water or in a sink filled with hot water; stir icing until it is just warmed and thin enough to pour easily. Use the icing immediately because it will set very quickly.

STORAGE Cake will keep for up to 3 days in an airtight container. Unfrosted cake can be frozen for up to 3 months.

cherry cake

The subtle richness of almonds is brilliant with nice-to-bite cherry chunks.

PREPARATION TIME 20 MINUTES BAKING TIME 1 HOUR 15 MINUTES

180g BUTTER, SOFTENED
1 TEASPOON ALMOND ESSENCE
165g CASTER SUGAR
3 EGGS
300g SELF-RAISING FLOUR
2 TABLESPOONS GROUND ALMONDS
80ml MILK
120ml SOURED CREAM
210g RED GLACÉ CHERRIES, QUARTERED

1 Grease deep 20cm (8in) round cake tin, line base with baking parchment; grease paper.
2 Beat butter, essence and sugar in small bowl with electric mixer until light and fluffy; add eggs 1 at a time, beating well after additions.
3 Stir in sifted flour and ground almonds in 2 batches with milk and soured cream; stir in cherries.
4 Spread mixture into prepared tin; bake in moderate oven about 1¼ hours. Stand cake 3 minutes before turning onto wire rack to cool. Sprinkle with sifted icing sugar, if desired.

SERVES 10

STORAGE Cake can be made a day ahead. Store in airtight container. Suitable for freezing

jam roll

PREPARATION TIME 20 MINUTES BAKING TIME 8 MINUTES

3 EGGS, SEPARATED
110g CASTER SUGAR
110g SELF-RAISING FLOUR
2 TABLESPOONS HOT MILK
110g CASTER SUGAR, EXTRA
160g JAM, WARMED

1 Position oven shelves; preheat oven to moderately hot. Grease 25cm x 30cm (10in x 12in) swiss roll tin; line base and short sides of pan with a strip of baking parchment, bringing parchment 5cm (2in) over edges, grease parchment.

2 Beat egg whites in small bowl with electric mixer until soft peaks form; gradually add sugar, 1 tablespoon at a time, beating until dissolved between additions.

3 With motor operating, add egg yolks, one at a time, beating until mixture is pale and thick; this will take about 10 minutes.

4 Meanwhile, sift flour three times onto baking parchment.

5 Pour hot milk down side of bowl; add triple-sifted flour. Working quickly, use plastic spatula to fold milk and flour through egg mixture. Pour mixture into prepared tin, gently spreading mixture evenly into corners.

6 Bake cake in moderately hot oven about 8 minutes or until top of cake feels soft and springy when touched lightly with fingertips.

7 Meanwhile, place a piece of baking parchment cut the same size as cake on board or bench; sprinkle evenly with extra sugar. When cooked, immediately turn cake onto sugared paper, quickly peeling away the lining paper. Working rapidly, use serrated knife to cut away crisp edges from all sides of cake.

8 Using hands, gently roll cake loosely from one of the short sides; unroll, spread evenly with jam.

9 Roll cake again, from same short side, by lifting paper and using it to guide the roll into shape.

10 Either serve jam roll immediately with cream, or place onto wire rack to cool.

SERVES 10

Trimming all sides of sponge

Rolling jam roll, using paper as guide

TIPS While this is easy to make, it may take a bit of experimentation with your oven to determine the best temperature and to perfect the timing – two elements that are critical for the success of this cake. Every oven is slightly different to another; be guided by the manufacturer's instructions for your oven. As a guide, the second shelf up from the oven floor is usually the best position for the cake tin and the temperature should be 200°C in a fan-assisted oven.

Gentle folding of the milk and flour through the egg mixture is also important for success; heavy handling of the mixture equals a heavy sponge cake. Use whatever kitchen tool you feel most comfortable with to incorporate the ingredients. Some people prefer to use a large metal spoon, some their hand or a rubber or plastic spatula; it doesn't matter what you use, it's how you use it that's important.

Jam can be warmed for about 20 seconds in a microwave oven on HIGH (100%).

STORAGE Cake must be made the day it is served.

Also known as a jelly roll in the United States, this filled and rolled sponge cake has long been a favourite in Britain, although its true origins are obscure. Quick and easy to make yet very impressive-looking, slices of the roll are good served warm or at room temperature with a dollop of whipped cream.

Using scissors, quarter cherries

Levelling cake mixture with wet spatula

cherry almond cake

PREPARATION TIME 20 MINUTES (PLUS STANDING TIME) BAKING TIME 1 HOUR 30 MINUTES

185g BUTTER, SOFTENED
220g CASTER SUGAR
1 TEASPOON ALMOND ESSENCE
3 EGGS
105g RED GLACÉ CHERRIES, QUARTERED
70g GREEN GLACÉ CHERRIES, QUARTERED
160g SULTANAS
90g SLIVERED ALMONDS
150g PLAIN FLOUR
75g SELF-RAISING FLOUR
80ml MILK

1 Position oven shelves; preheat oven to moderately low. Line base and side of deep 20cm (8in) round cake tin with three thicknesses baking parchment, extending parchment 5cm (2in) above edge of tin.
2 Combine butter, sugar and essence in small bowl; beat with electric mixer until light and fluffy. Add eggs, one at a time, beating well between additions. Mixture may curdle at this point but will come together later.
3 Combine cherries, sultanas and nuts in large bowl; using wooden spoon, stir in creamed mixture, flours and milk. Spread mixture into prepared tin, level surface with wet metal spatula.
4 Bake cake in moderately low oven about 1½ hours.
5 Cover tin tightly with foil; cool cake in tin.

SERVES 22

GLACE CHERRIES are boiled in heavy sugar syrup, then dried to make these beautiful, sweet and colourful baubles. There is no difference in the flavour between the green, red or yellow cherries, but the different colours add decoration to the cake when cut.

STORAGE Remove cake from tin; wrap cake tightly in cling film to keep airtight, then in foil. Wrapped cake can be kept in a cool, dark place for about 2 weeks; however, if the climate is humid, keep the cake in a sealed plastic bag or tightly sealed container in the refrigerator. Cake can be frozen for up to 3 months.

TIPS Cover cake loosely with foil during baking if it starts to overbrown.

Give the cake quarter turns several times during baking to help to avoid it browning unevenly.

Almond essence is available from supermarkets and health food stores.

date, ricotta & polenta cake

PREPARATION TIME 30 MINUTES BAKING TIME 1 HOUR 45 MINUTES

160g FINELY CHOPPED STONED DATES
80ml GRAND MARNIER
60g UNROASTED HAZELNUTS
300g SELF-RAISING FLOUR
1 TEASPOON BAKING POWDER
110g POLENTA
220g CASTER SUGAR
250g RICOTTA CHEESE
125g BUTTER, MELTED
180ml WATER

RICOTTA FILLING
250g RICOTTA CHEESE
2 TABLESPOONS GRAND MARNIER
2 TABLESPOONS ICING SUGAR
1 TABLESPOON FINELY GRATED ORANGE RIND

Polenta is the coarsely ground yellow cornmeal used for making cornmeal muffins and cornbread; it gives this cake a particularly dense texture. This is the perfect cake to serve at the end of an Italian meal, or with a cup of espresso when friends drop by in the late afternoon.

1 Position oven shelves; preheat oven to moderately low. Grease deep 22cm (9in) round cake tin; line base and side with baking parchment.
2 Combine dates and liqueur in small bowl; stand 15 minutes.
3 Meanwhile, roast nuts on oven tray in moderate oven about 10 minutes; wrap warm nuts in tea-towel, rub to remove skins. Chop nuts coarsely.
4 Combine flour, baking powder, polenta, sugar, cheese, butter and the water in large bowl; beat on low speed with electric mixer until just combined. Beat on medium speed until mixture changes to a lighter colour then, using wooden spoon, stir in nuts and undrained date mixture.
5 Spread half of the cake mixture into prepared tin; using metal spatula, spread ricotta filling over tin mixture then cover with remaining cake mixture.
6 Bake cake in moderately low oven 45 minutes; cover tightly with foil, bake about 1 hour. Discard foil, stand cake in tin 10 minutes then turn onto wire rack; turn top-side up to cool.

RICOTTA FILLING Combine ingredients in medium bowl, stir with wooden spoon until smooth.

SERVES 16

Rubbing skins off roasted hazelnuts

Coarsely chopping nuts

TIPS Chopped seeded prunes or raisins can be substituted for the dates.
Brandy, rum, or your favourite liqueur can be substituted for Grand Marnier, and you can substitute the hazelnuts with any other variety of nut you like. Just be certain that you select a citrus fruit that complements the flavour of the liqueur and nuts you choose. For example, Cointreau, lemon rind and walnuts marry well, as do brandy, mandarin and pecans.

STORAGE Cake will keep for up to 3 days in an airtight container at room temperature.

TIPS Easy to make as it's mixed in just one bowl, this moist cake has a real lemony flavour and keeps well.

STORAGE Cake can be made a week ahead; store in an airtight container.

lemon sour cream cake

PREPARATION TIME 35 MINUTES COOKING TIME 1 HOUR 30 MINUTES (PLUS COOLING TIME)

250g BUTTER, SOFTENED
2 TABLESPOONS GRATED LEMON RIND
440g CASTER SUGAR
6 EGGS
300g PLAIN FLOUR
35g SELF-RAISING FLOUR
180g SOURED CREAM

1 Preheat oven to moderately low (170°C/150°C fan-assisted). Grease deep 27cm (11in) round cake tin; line base with baking parchment.

2 Beat butter, rind and sugar in large bowl with electric mixer until light and fluffy; beat in eggs one at a time. Stir in half the sifted flours and half the soured cream, then stir in remaining flours and remaining soured cream until smooth.

3 Spread mixture into tin; bake about 1½ hours. Stand cake 5 minutes before turning onto wire rack to cool. Dust with sifted icing sugar before serving, if desired.

SERVES 12

moist coconut cake with coconut ice frosting

PREPARATION TIME 25 MINUTES COOKING TIME 1 HOUR (PLUS COOLING TIME)

125g BUTTER, SOFTENED
½ TEASPOON COCONUT ESSENCE
220g CASTER SUGAR
2 EGGS
40g DESICCATED COCONUT
225g SELF-RAISING FLOUR
300g SOURED CREAM
80ml MILK

COCONUT ICE FROSTING
320g ICING SUGAR
110g DESICCATED COCONUT
2 EGG WHITES, BEATEN LIGHTLY
PINK FOOD COLOURING

1 Preheat oven to moderate (180°C/160°C fan-assisted). Grease deep 22cm (9in) round cake tin; line base with baking parchment.
2 Beat butter, essence and sugar in small bowl with electric mixer until light and fluffy. Beat in eggs, one at a time.
3 Transfer mixture to large bowl. Stir in half the coconut and half the sifted flour, half the sour cream and half the milk, then add remaining coconut, flour, sour cream and milk; stir until smooth.
4 Spread mixture into tin; bake about 1 hour. Stand cake in tin 5 minutes before turning onto wire rack to cool.
5 Meanwhile, make coconut ice frosting.
6 Top cold cake with coconut ice frosting.

COCONUT ICE FROSTING Combine sifted icing sugar in bowl with coconut and egg whites; mix well. Tint pink with a little colouring.

SERVES 10

TIPS While this is easy to make, it may take a bit of experimentation with your oven to determine the best temperature and to perfect the timing – two elements that are critical for the success of this sponge cake. Every oven is slightly different to another; be guided by your oven manufacturer's instructions. As a guide, the second shelf up from the oven floor is usually the best position for the cake tin and the temperature should be 200°C in a fan-assisted oven.

Gentle folding of the water and flour mixtures through the egg mixture is also important for success; heavy handling of the mixture equals a heavy sponge cake.

Use whatever kitchen tool you feel most comfortable with to incorporate the ingredients. Some people prefer to use a large metal spoon, some their hand or a rubber or plastic spatula: it doesn't matter what you use, it's how you use it.

Mock cream is a smooth mixture suitable for cream buns and other similar cakes but not thick enough to use for piping. It should not be refrigerated; because of the butter content, it will become rock hard. Cake can be filled up to 2 hours before required.

STORAGE Cake is best made on the day it is to be served.

perfect honey roll

PREPARATION TIME 20 MINUTES BAKING TIME 15 MINUTES

1 EGG, SEPARATED
3 EGG WHITES
2 TABLESPOONS TREACLE
175g GOLDEN SYRUP
75g CORNFLOUR
50g SELF-RAISING FLOUR
1 TEASPOON GROUND GINGER
1 TEASPOON GROUND CINNAMON
½ TEASPOON GROUND NUTMEG
¼ TEASPOON GROUND CLOVE
2 TABLESPOONS BOILING WATER
½ TEASPOON BICARBONATE OF SODA
30g DESICCATED COCONUT

MOCK CREAM
110g CASTER SUGAR
½ TEASPOON GELATINE
1 TABLESPOON MILK
80ml WATER
125g BUTTER, SOFTENED
½ TEASPOON VANILLA ESSENCE

1 Position oven shelves; preheat oven to hot. Grease 25cm x 30cm (10in x 12in) swiss roll tin; line base and short sides with baking parchment, bringing parchment 5cm (2in) over edges. Grease the baking parchment.
2 Beat the four egg whites in small bowl with electric mixer until soft peaks form; with motor operating, gradually add combined treacle and golden syrup in a thin stream.
3 Add egg yolk; beat until pale and thick. Transfer mixture to large bowl; using a metal spoon, fold in combined triple-sifted flours and spices, and combined water and soda. Pour mixture into prepared tin; gently spreading mixture evenly into corners.
4 Bake cake in hot oven about 15 minutes.
5 Meanwhile, place a piece of baking parchment cut slightly larger than the cake on bench; sprinkle evenly with coconut. When cake is cooked, turn immediately onto paper, quickly peeling away the lining paper. Working rapidly, use serrated knife to carefully cut away crisp edges from all sides of cake.
6 Carefully roll cake loosely from one short side by lifting paper and using it to guide roll into shape; stand 10 seconds then unroll. Re-roll cake; cool to room temperature.
7 Gently unroll cake, spread with mock cream, carefully re-roll cake.

MOCK CREAM Combine sugar, gelatine, milk and water in small saucepan; stir over low heat, without boiling, until sugar and gelatine dissolve. Cool to room temperature. Beat butter and essence in small bowl with electric mixer until white and fluffy. With motor operating, gradually beat in sugar mixture until fluffy; this will take up to 15 minutes. Mock cream thickens on standing.

SERVES 8

Trimming edges of sponge

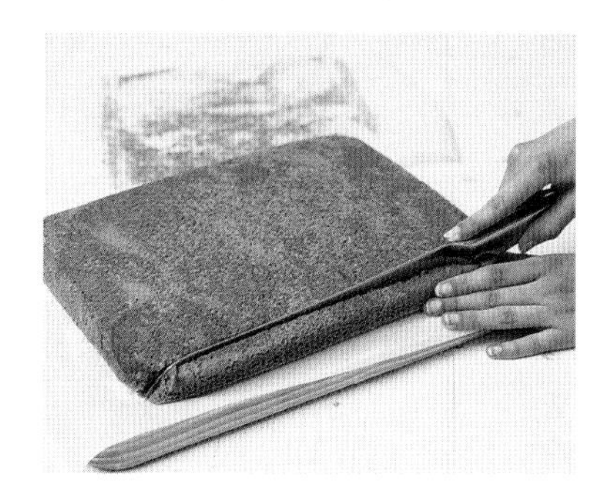

Rolling sponge in baking paper

Spreading sponge with mock cream

STORAGE Can be made 2 days ahead; keep in an airtight container.

moist orange cake

PREPARATION TIME 25 MINUTES COOKING TIME 45 MINUTES (PLUS COOLING TIME)

155g BUTTER, SOFTENED
2 TEASPOONS FINELY GRATED ORANGE RIND
150g CASTER SUGAR
3 EGGS
185g SELF-RAISING FLOUR
60ml MILK
1 TABLESPOON DESICCATED COCONUT

ORANGE ICING
160g ICING SUGAR
1 TEASPOON BUTTER, SOFTENED
1 TABLESPOON ORANGE JUICE, APPROXIMATELY

1 Preheat oven to moderate (180°C/160°C fan-assisted). Grease deep 20cm (8in) round cake tin; line base with baking parchment.
2 Combine butter, rind, sugar, eggs, sifted flour and milk in large bowl; beat on low speed with electric mixer until combined. Increase speed to medium, beat about 3 minutes or until mixture is lighter in colour and smooth.
3 Spread mixture into tin; bake about 45 minutes. Stand cake in tin 5 minutes before turning onto wire rack to cool.
4 Meanwhile, make orange icing.
5 Spread cold cake with orange icing; sprinkle with coconut.

ORANGE ICING Sift icing sugar into small heatproof bowl, stir in butter and enough juice to make a stiff paste. Stir over hot water until icing is spreadable.

SERVES 8

apricot chocolate chip cake

PREPARATION TIME 30 MINUTES (PLUS STANDING TIME)
COOKING TIME 1 HOUR 15 MINUTES (PLUS COOKING TIME)

150g CHOPPED DRIED APRICOTS
250ml APRICOT NECTAR
125g BUTTER, SOFTENED
150g RAW SUGAR
2 EGGS, SEPARATED
120g DESICCATED COCONUT
225g SELF-RAISING FLOUR
95g DARK CHOCOLATE CHIPS

1 Preheat oven to moderate (180°C/160°C fan-assisted). Grease deep 20cm (8in) round cake tin; line base with baking parchment.
2 Combine apricots and nectar in medium bowl; stand 1 hour.
3 Beat butter and sugar in small bowl with electric mixer until light and fluffy. Add egg yolks, beat until combined.
4 Transfer mixture to large bowl, stir in coconut then half the sifted flour and half the apricot mixture. Stir in remaining flour, remaining apricot mixture then chocolate chips.
5 Beat egg whites in small bowl with electric mixer until soft peaks form; fold into apricot mixture.
6 Spread mixture into tin; bake about 1¼ hours. Stand cake 5 minutes before turning onto wire rack to cool.
7 Serve cake dusted with sifted icing sugar, if desired.

SERVES 8

TIP Apricot nectar is the juice of apricots. If you can't find the juice in the supermarket, buy tinned apricots and blend them to a pulp.

STORAGE Cake can be kept for up to 3 days stored in an airtight container.

raspberry & coconut muffins

PREPARATION TIME 10 MINUTES BAKING TIME 20 MINUTES

375g SELF-RAISING FLOUR
90g BUTTER, CHOPPED
220g CASTER SUGAR
310ml BUTTERMILK
1 EGG, BEATEN LIGHTLY
30g DESICCATED COCONUT
150g FRESH OR FROZEN RASPBERRIES
2 TABLESPOONS SHREDDED COCONUT

1 Position oven shelves; preheat oven to moderately hot. Grease 12-hole (80ml) muffin tray.
2 Place flour in large bowl; using fingertips, rub in butter. Add sugar, buttermilk, egg, desiccated coconut and raspberries; using fork, mix until just combined.
3 Divide mixture among holes of prepared tray; sprinkle with shredded coconut.
4 Bake in moderately hot oven about 20 minutes. Stand muffins 5 minutes then turn onto wire rack to cool.

MAKES 12

Stirring ingredients together

Sprinkling coconut over muffin mixture

TIPS It is important not to overmix the muffin mixture; it should be slightly lumpy.
■ If using frozen berries, use them unthawed, this will minimise 'bleeding' of the colour into the mixture.
■ To thaw frozen muffins, either place muffins on an oven tray covered with foil, or wrap individual muffins in foil; thaw in moderate oven about 20 minutes.
■ Individual unwrapped muffins can be thawed in a microwave oven on HIGH (100%) for about 30 seconds.
■ Traditionally, these American muffins are served warm with butter.

STORAGE Muffins are at their best made on the day of serving; however, they can be stored in an airtight container for up to 2 days. Muffins can be frozen either individually wrapped in foil or together in a sealed container for up to 3 months.

TIP You can melt the butter in a microwave.

STORAGE These friands can be made 2 days ahead. Recipe suitable to freeze.

little lime friands

Friands, known as financiers in France, are little moist little cakes made with ground almonds. You can buy special friand moulds, but they work almost as well in mini muffin trays.

6 EGG WHITES
185g BUTTER, MELTED
125g GROUND ALMONDS
240g ICING SUGAR
75g PLAIN FLOUR
1 TABLESPOON FINELY GRATED LIME RIND
1 TABLESPOON LIME JUICE
30 WHOLE BLANCHED ALMONDS (60g)

PREPARATION TIME 20 MINUTES COOKING TIME 15 MINUTES (PLUS COOLING TIME)

1 Preheat oven to moderately hot. Grease 30 1½-tablespoon (30ml) mini muffin tray holes.
2 Place egg whites in medium bowl; whisk lightly until combined. Add butter, ground almonds, sifted icing sugar and flour, then rind and juice. Whisk until just combined. Divide mixture among prepared trays; top mixture in each hole with an almond.
3 Bake in moderately hot oven about 15 minutes. Turn onto wire racks to cool, right way up. Serve warm or at room temperature.

MAKES 30

walnut brownie bites

PREPARATION TIME 15 MINUTES (PLUS STANDING TIME)
COOKING TIME 20 MINUTES (PLUS COOLING TIME)

50g WALNUTS, TOASTED, CHOPPED FINELY
80g BUTTER
150g DARK CHOCOLATE, CHOPPED COARSELY
150g FIRMLY PACKED BROWN SUGAR
1 EGG, BEATEN LIGHTLY
50g PLAIN FLOUR
60g SOURED CREAM
3 X 50g PACKETS ROLOS

1 Preheat oven to moderate. Lightly grease two non-stick 12-hole 1½-tablespoon (30ml) mini muffin trays; divide walnuts among holes.
2 Stir butter and chocolate in small saucepan over low heat until smooth. Stir in sugar; cool to just warm.
3 Stir in egg, then flour and soured cream; spoon mixture into prepared trays. Press one Rolo into centre of each quantity of mixture; spread mixture so that Rolo is completely enclosed. Bake in moderate oven 15 minutes. Using a sharp-pointed knife, loosen sides of brownies from tray; stand 10 minutes. Remove brownies gently from tray.

MAKES 24

TIP These treats are best served while still warm.

TIPS Cake mixture can also be baked in a deep 19cm (7½in) square or deep 22cm (9in) round cake tin; baking time will increase to about 2¼ hours. Line base and sides of larger tins with three thicknesses baking parchment, bringing paper 5cm (2in) above edge of tin.

■ Rum, sherry or your favourite liqueur can be substituted for the brandy.

■ Use a light-flavoured all-purpose vegetable oil, such as rapeseed, in this recipe.

Sifting dry ingredients over fruit mixture

Dividing cake mixture among tins

quick-mix low-fat fruit cakes

PREPARATION TIME 25 MINUTES (PLUS STANDING TIME)
BAKING TIME 1 HOUR 45 MINUTES

750g MIXED DRIED FRUIT
105g RED GLACÉ CHERRIES, QUARTERED
150g FIRMLY PACKED BROWN SUGAR
375ml APPLE JUICE
2 EGG WHITES, BEATEN LIGHTLY
60ml VEGETABLE OIL
80ml SKIMMED MILK
2 TABLESPOONS BRANDY
360g WHOLEMEAL SELF-RAISING FLOUR
1 TEASPOON MIXED SPICE
½ TEASPOON GROUND GINGER
1 TABLESPOON BRANDY, EXTRA

These cakes make a great gift for any weight-conscious friends or family members because of their comparatively low fat content.

1 Combine fruit, cherries, sugar and juice in large bowl, cover; stand overnight.
2 Position oven shelves; preheat oven to low. Grease seven 8.5cm (3½in) round cake tins; line bases with three thicknesses baking parchment.
3 Using wooden spoon, stir egg white, oil, milk, brandy and sifted dry ingredients into fruit mixture. Divide mixture evenly among prepared tins.
4 Bake cakes in low oven about 1¾ hours. Brush hot cakes with extra brandy. Cover tins tightly with foil; cool cakes in tins.
5 Decorate cakes with star shapes cut from rolled almond paste, if desired; position stars on cakes, decorate with silver, gold or coloured cachous.

SERVES 21

STORAGE Wrap cakes tightly in cling film to keep airtight; refrigerate in airtight container for up to 1 month. Cakes can be frozen for up to 3 months.

TIP The caramel filling and chocolate are suitable to microwave.

STORAGE These tarts can be made 3 days ahead and stored in an airtight container.

caramel chocolate tarts

PREPARATION TIME 25 MINUTES (PLUS STANDING TIME)
COOKING TIME 15 MINUTES (PLUS COOLING TIME)

150g PLAIN FLOUR
90g BUTTER, CHOPPED
55g CASTER SUGAR
100g DARK CHOCOLATE, MELTED

CARAMEL FILLING
395g CAN SWEETENED CONDENSED MILK
30g BUTTER, CHOPPED
2 TABLESPOONS GOLDEN SYRUP

1 Preheat oven to moderate. Grease two 12-hole 1-tablespoon (30ml) mini muffin trays.
2 Sift flour into medium bowl. Rub in butter; stir in sugar. Press 2 teaspoons of the mixture into each hole of muffin trays. Bake in moderate oven about 10 minutes or until browned lightly.
3 Pour hot caramel filling over hot bases; return to oven 3 minutes. Stand tarts 2 minutes before gently removing from pans; cool.
4 Spread top of tarts with chocolate; stand at room temperature until set.

CARAMEL FILLING Combine ingredients in small saucepan; stir over low heat until butter melts and mixture is combined.

MAKES 24

amaretti

PREPARATION TIME 15 MINUTES (PLUS STANDING TIME)
COOKING TIME 15 MINUTES

125g GROUND ALMONDS
220g CASTER SUGAR
2 LARGE EGG WHITES
½ TEASPOON VANILLA ESSENCE
2 DROPS ALMOND ESSENCE
20 BLANCHED ALMONDS

1 Beat ground almonds, sugar, egg whites and essences in medium bowl with electric mixer, on medium speed, 3 minutes; stand 5 minutes.
2 Spoon mixture into piping bag fitted with 1cm (½in) plain tube; pipe in circular motion from centre, to make biscuits about 4cm (1½in) in diameter leaving 2cm (¾in) between each. Top with almonds.
3 Bake, uncovered, in moderate oven, about 12 minutes or until tops are browned lightly. Stand on trays 5 minutes before removing with metal spatula. Cool on wire rack.

MAKES 20

STORAGE Amaretti can be made 3 days ahead and stored in airtight container.

TIPS Sicilian creams are best assembled close to serving.
■ Any liqueur can be used to flavour these biscuits, e.g. Galliano, Grand Marnier, Cointreau or Amaretto.

sicilian creams

PREPARATION TIME 35 MINUTES COOKING TIME 20 MINUTES (PLUS COOLING TIME)

260g SELF-RAISING FLOUR
60g BUTTER
110g CASTER SUGAR
1 TEASPOON GRATED LEMON RIND
1 TEASPOON VANILLA ESSENCE
1 EGG
60ml MILK
60ml CREAM
2 TABLESPOONS ICING SUGAR
1 TABLESPOON WATER
1 TABLESPOON LIQUEUR
1 TABLESPOON ICING SUGAR, EXTRA

1 Place flour in large bowl; rub in butter. Add sugar; mix well. Make well in centre of mixture; add combined rind, vanilla, egg and milk. Using wooden spoon, mix to a soft, pliable dough.
2 Turn dough onto lightly floured surface; knead gently until smooth. Dough should be soft and pliable.
3 Roll dough out gently until 1cm (½in) thick. Cut into rounds using 5cm (2in) cutter; place on lightly greased oven trays, about 2.5cm (1in) apart. Bake, uncovered, in moderate oven about 15 minutes or until light golden brown; cool on wire rack. [Can be made 2 days ahead to this stage and refrigerated, covered.]
4 Beat cream and icing sugar in small bowl with electric mixer until firm peaks form. Using fine serrated knife, split each biscuit in half, horizontally; brush cut side of each top half of biscuit with combined water and liqueur. Join biscuits with cream filling; dust with extra icing sugar.

MAKES 12

panettone custards with macadamia toffee

PREPARATION TIME 20 MINUTES COOKING TIME 40 MINUTES (PLUS STANDING TIME)

500g PANETTONE
50g SOFTENED BUTTER
875ml MILK
1 VANILLA POD, HALVED LENGTHWAYS
4 EGGS
220g SUGAR
110g MACADAMIA NUTS, CHOPPED COARSELY
2 TABLESPOONS WATER
2 TEASPOONS ICING SUGAR

1 Grease six 250ml ovenproof dishes.
2 Cut panettone into 1.5cm (¾in) thick rounds; spread one side of each round with butter. Cut each round into quarters; divide among prepared dishes.
3 Combine milk and vanilla pod in medium saucepan; bring almost to a boil. Remove from heat; stand, covered, 10 minutes.
4 Meanwhile, whisk eggs and half of the sugar in large heatproof jug. Gradually whisk hot milk mixture into egg mixture. Strain into large jug; discard vanilla pod.
5 Carefully pour egg mixture over panettone in prepared dishes. Place dishes in large baking dish; add enough boiling water to come halfway up sides of dishes. Bake, uncovered, in moderately low oven about 30 minutes or until set.
6 Meanwhile, place nuts on oven tray; toast, uncovered, in oven with panettone about 10 minutes or until browned lightly. Place remaining sugar and the water in small saucepan; stir over heat, without boiling, until sugar dissolves. Boil, uncovered, without stirring, about 10 minutes or until sugar syrup is golden brown; pour over nuts. Cool; chop toffee coarsely.
7 Serve custards topped with toffee; dust tops lightly with icing sugar.

SERVES 6

TIP Brioche, hot cross buns or fruit loaf can be used instead of the panettone.

PANETTONE is an Italian cake made with yeast and containing dried fruit, traditionally eaten at Christmas and Easter. It's traditionally baked in a deep mould to give it height. Panettone can be served as a dessert, accompanied by a sweet wine such as Marsala, and is also delicious toasted and buttered, or, as in this recipe, used in place of bread in a bread and butter pudding.

slices & cookies to share

coco-berry-nut squares

PREPARATION TIME 20 MINUTES BAKING TIME 50 MINUTES

250g BUTTER, SOFTENED
1 TEASPOON VANILLA ESSENCE
275g CASTER SUGAR
3 EGGS
100g PLAIN FLOUR
150g SELF-RAISING FLOUR
55g GROUND HAZELNUTS
150g FROZEN RASPBERRIES

COCONUT TOPPING
50g PLAIN FLOUR
2 TABLESPOONS CASTER SUGAR
40g BUTTER
15g FLAKED COCONUT, CHOPPED COARSELY

1 Position oven shelves; preheat oven to moderate. Grease deep 23cm (9in) square cake tin; line base with baking parchment.
2 Beat butter, essence and sugar in small bowl with electric mixer until light and fluffy; beat in eggs, one at a time, until just combined between additions.
3 Transfer mixture to large bowl; using wooden spoon, stir in flours and ground hazelnuts.
4 Spread mixture evenly into prepared tin; sprinkle evenly with raspberries, then the coconut topping.
5 Bake cake in moderate oven about 50 minutes. Stand cake 5 minutes then turn onto wire rack; turn cake top-side up to cool. Cut into squares before serving.

COCONUT TOPPING Combine flour and sugar in small bowl. Rub in butter; using fork, stir in coconut.

SERVES 12

These lusciously moist squares come straight from the oven with their own baked-on topping – but a dollop of whipped cream on a warm piece won't go astray!

TIPS Cover cake loosely with foil if it starts to overbrown during baking.
■ It is best to use still-frozen raspberries. You can also use fresh raspberries, but avoid using very large berries because they have a tendency to sink into the cake mixture.
■ Fresh or frozen blueberries can be substituted for the raspberries.
■ Ground almonds can be substituted for ground hazelnuts.

STORAGE Squares will keep for 1 day in an airtight container in the refrigerator. Squares can be frozen for up to 3 months.

caramel & chocolate slices

PREPARATION TIME 20 MINUTES COOKING TIME 25 MINUTES (PLUS COOLING TIME)

75g PLAIN FLOUR
75g SELF-RAISING FLOUR
90g ROLLED OATS
165g FIRMLY PACKED BROWN SUGAR
150g BUTTER, MELTED
125g DARK EATING CHOCOLATE, CHOPPED COARSELY
55g COARSELY CHOPPED WALNUTS
35g PLAIN FLOUR, EXTRA
125ml CARAMEL TOPPING

1 Preheat oven to moderate (180°C/160°C fan-assisted). Grease 19cm x 29cm (7½in x 11½in) rectangular slice tin; line base and two long sides with baking parchment, extending paper 2cm (¾in) above edges.
2 Combine flours, oats and sugar in medium bowl, stir in butter. Press half the mixture into tin. Bake 10 minutes. Remove from oven, sprinkle with chocolate and walnuts.
3 Blend extra flour with caramel topping in small bowl. Drizzle evenly over chocolate and walnuts, then sprinkle with remaining oat mixture.
4 Bake further 15 minutes. Cool in tin; cut into squares or slices before serving.

MAKES 15

TIP We used a thick, caramel-flavoured ice-cream topping in this recipe.

sweet coconut squares

PREPARATION TIME 40 MINUTES (PLUS REFRIGERATION TIME)
COOKING TIME 40 MINUTES (PLUS COOLING TIME)

STORAGE Store squares in airtight container for up to 4 days. Cooked squares are suitable to freeze, covered, for up to 2 weeks. Thaw at room temperature.

150g PLAIN FLOUR
75g SELF-RAISING FLOUR
2 TABLESPOONS CASTER SUGAR
125g CHILLED BUTTER, CHOPPED
1 EGG
1 TABLESPOON ICED WATER
160g APRICOT JAM
10 RED GLACÉ CHERRIES, HALVED

COCONUT FILLING
250ml WATER
220g CASTER SUGAR
280g DESICCATED COCONUT
3 EGGS, BEATEN LIGHTLY
60g BUTTER, MELTED
60ml MILK
1 TEASPOON VANILLA EXTRACT
1 TEASPOON BAKING POWDER

1 Blend or process flours, sugar and butter until combined. Add egg and the water, process until mixture forms a ball; cover, refrigerate 30 minutes.
2 Meanwhile, make coconut filling.
3 Preheat oven to moderate (180°C/160°C fan-assisted). Line 25cm x 30cm (10in x 12in) swiss roll tin with baking parchment, extending paper 5cm (2in) over long sides.
4 Roll pastry between sheets of baking parchment until 3mm thick and large enough to cover base of tin. Gently ease into base of tin.
5 Brush jam evenly over pastry. Spread coconut mixture over jam.
6 Place cherry halves evenly over slice top. Bake about 35 minutes. Cool in tin; cut into squares before serving.

MAKES 20

COCONUT FILLING Combine the water and sugar in small saucepan, stir over heat until sugar is dissolved. Bring to a boil, boil 3 minutes without stirring; cool sugar syrup 5 minutes. Place coconut in large bowl, stir in sugar syrup, egg, butter, milk, extract and baking powder.

A hit with every coconut lover, these squares just improve with age. The recipe can also be made as tartlets.

These slices are divine. They taste great on their own or even better when served warm with ice-cream.

flourless hazelnut chocolate slices

PREPARATION TIME 20 MINUTES COOKING TIME 1 HOUR (PLUS STANDING AND COOLING TIME)

35g COCOA POWDER
80ml HOT WATER
150g DARK EATING CHOCOLATE, MELTED
150g BUTTER, MELTED
295g FIRMLY PACKED BROWN SUGAR
100g GROUND HAZELNUTS
4 EGGS, SEPARATED
1 TABLESPOON COCOA POWDER, EXTRA

1 Preheat oven to moderate (180°C/160°C fan-assisted). Grease deep 19cm (7½in) square cake tin; line base and sides with baking parchment.
2 Blend cocoa with the hot water in large bowl until smooth. Stir in chocolate, butter, sugar, ground hazelnuts and egg yolks.
3 Beat egg whites in small bowl with electric mixer until soft peaks form; fold into chocolate mixture in two batches.
4 Pour mixture into tin; bake about 1 hour or until firm. Stand cake 15 minutes; turn, top-side up, onto wire rack to cool. Dust with sifted extra cocoa; cut into slices before serving.

SERVES 9

TIP Ground hazelnuts replace the flour in this recipe.

STORAGE These slices can be made up to 4 days in advance; keep, covered, in refrigerator. Slices can also be frozen for up to 3 months.

chewy choc-chunk cookies

PREPARATION TIME 25 MINUTES (PLUS REFRIGERATION TIME)
COOKING TIME 10 MINUTES PER TRAY (PLUS COOLING TIME)

2 EGGS
295g FIRMLY PACKED BROWN SUGAR
1 TEASPOON VANILLA EXTRACT
150g PLAIN FLOUR
110g SELF-RAISING FLOUR
½ TEASPOON BICARBONATE OF SODA
125ml VEGETABLE OIL
120g COARSELY CHOPPED TOASTED PECANS
120g COARSELY CHOPPED RAISINS
150g DARK EATING CHOCOLATE, CHOPPED COARSELY
95g WHITE CHOC CHIPS

1 Preheat oven to moderately hot (200°C/180°C fan-assisted). Grease baking trays.
2 Beat eggs, sugar and extract in small bowl with electric mixer about 1 minute or until mixture lightens in colour.
3 Stir in sifted dry ingredients then remaining ingredients (the mixture will be soft). Cover bowl; refrigerate 1 hour.
4 Roll heaped tablespoons of the mixture into balls; place onto trays about 6cm (2½in) apart, flatten into 6cm (2½in) rounds.
5 Bake about 10 minutes or until browned lightly. Stand cookies on baking trays 5 minutes; transfer to wire rack to cool.

MAKES 20

TIP Walnuts can be substituted for pecans, if desired.

STORAGE Cookies can be made up to 1 week ahead; keep in an airtight container.

Pressing base of cake into tin

Pouring topping mixture over base

nutmeg & cardamom spice slices

PREPARATION TIME 15 MINUTES
BAKING TIME 1 HOUR

150g SELF-RAISING FLOUR
150g PLAIN FLOUR
250g FIRMLY PACKED BROWN SUGAR
1 TEASPOON GROUND CINNAMON
½ TEASPOON GROUND NUTMEG
½ TEASPOON GROUND CARDAMOM
¼ TEASPOON GROUND CLOVES
125g BUTTER, CHOPPED
1 EGG
1 TEASPOON BICARBONATE OF SODA
180ml MILK
75g SHELLED UNSALTED PISTACHIOS, CHOPPED COARSELY

1 Position oven shelves; preheat oven to moderate. Grease 20cm x 30cm (8in x 12in) slice tin; line base and long sides of tin with baking parchment.
2 Blend or process flours, sugar, spices and butter until ingredients resemble fine breadcrumbs. Transfer mixture to medium bowl.
3 Firmly press 275g of the flour mixture evenly over base of prepared tin.
4 Use fork to combine egg, soda and milk in jug; add to remaining flour mixture with nuts, mix well with wooden spoon. Pour mixture over base in tin.
5 Bake cake in moderate oven about 1 hour. Stand cake 10 minutes then turn onto wire rack; turn cake top-side up to cool. Cut into slices before serving.

SERVES 15

NUTMEG A strong and very pungent spice ground from the dried nut of an evergreen tree native to Indonesia. Usually found ground, but the flavour is more intense from a whole nut, available from spice shops, so it's best to grate your own.

CARDAMOM Native to India and purchased in pod, seed or ground form, cardamom has a distinctive aromatic, sweetly rich flavour.

TIPS Any nuts, such as almonds, pecans, walnuts or hazelnuts, can be substituted for the pistachios.
- Butter should be chopped while still refrigerator-cold.
- Using a medium- to large-sized food processor or large blender will help make mixing of the butter through the dry ingredients quicker and easier; an alternative, however, is to finely chop or coarsely grate the cold butter then rub it through the dry ingredients with your fingertips.

STORAGE Slices can be kept in an airtight container for up to 3 days. Slices can be frozen for up to 1 month.

vanilla currant cookies

125g BUTTER, SOFTENED
1 TEASPOON VANILLA EXTRACT
165g CASTER SUGAR
1 EGG
300g SELF-RAISING FLOUR
40g DESICCATED COCONUT
40g CURRANTS

VANILLA ICING
240g ICING SUGAR
2 TEASPOONS VANILLA EXTRACT
1½ TEASPOONS BUTTER, SOFTENED
1 TABLESPOON MILK, APPROXIMATELY

STORAGE Cookies can be made up to 2 weeks ahead; store in an airtight container.

PREPARATION TIME 45 MINUTES COOKING TIME 10 MINUTES PER TRAY (PLUS COOLING TIME)

1 Preheat oven to moderately hot (200°C/180°C fan-assisted). Grease baking trays.
2 Beat butter, extract, sugar and egg in small bowl with electric mixer until light and fluffy. Transfer mixture to large bowl, stir in sifted flour, coconut and currants.
3 Shape rounded teaspoons of mixture into balls; place onto trays about 5cm (2in) apart. Flatten with hand until about 5mm (¼in) thick.
4 Bake about 10 minutes or until browned lightly. Cool on trays.
5 Spread cookies thinly with vanilla icing, place on wire racks to set.

VANILLA ICING Sift icing sugar into medium heatproof bowl, stir in extract and butter, then enough milk to give a thick paste. Stir over hot water until spreadable.

MAKES 40

TIPS Other nuts, such as walnuts or pecans, can be used instead of macadamias.

STORAGE Cookies can be made up to 1 week ahead; store in an airtight container.

fudgy-wudgy chocolate cookies

PREPARATION TIME 15 MINUTES COOKING TIME 10 MINUTES (PLUS COOLING TIME)

125g BUTTER, CHOPPED
1 TEASPOON VANILLA EXTRACT
275g FIRMLY PACKED BROWN SUGAR
1 EGG
150g PLAIN FLOUR
35g SELF-RAISING FLOUR
1 TEASPOON BICARBONATE OF SODA
35g COCOA POWDER
75g RAISINS
110g MACADAMIA NUTS, TOASTED, CHOPPED COARSELY
95g DARK CHOC CHIPS
75g DARK EATING CHOCOLATE, CHOPPED COARSELY

1 Preheat oven to moderate (180°C/160°C fan-assisted). Line three baking trays with baking parchment.
2 Beat butter, extract, sugar and egg in medium bowl with electric mixer until smooth. Stir in sifted flours, bicarbonate of soda and cocoa powder; stir in raisins, nuts and both chocolates.
3 Drop rounded tablespoons of mixture onto trays about 4cm (1½in) apart; press each with hand to flatten slightly.
4 Bake 10 minutes. Stand cookies on trays 5 minutes; transfer to wire rack to cool.

MAKES 24

STORAGE Slices can be kept up to 1 week in an airtight container in the refrigerator. Slices can be frozen for up to 3 months.

lumberjack slices

PREPARATION TIME 30 MINUTES BAKING TIME 1 HOUR 10 MINUTES

2 LARGE APPLES (400g), PEELED, CORED, FINELY CHOPPED
200g FINELY CHOPPED STONED DRIED DATES
1 TEASPOON BICARBONATE OF SODA
250ml BOILING WATER
125g BUTTER, SOFTENED
1 TEASPOON VANILLA ESSENCE
220g CASTER SUGAR
1 EGG
225g PLAIN FLOUR

TOPPING
60g BUTTER
100g FIRMLY PACKED BROWN SUGAR
125ml MILK
50g SHREDDED COCONUT

1 Position oven shelves; preheat oven to moderate. Grease deep 23cm (9in) square cake tin; line base and sides with baking parchment.
2 Combine apple, dates and soda in large bowl, add the water, cover bowl with cling film; stand 10 minutes.
3 Meanwhile, beat butter, essence, sugar and egg in small bowl with electric mixer until light and fluffy.
4 Add creamed butter mixture to apple mixture; using wooden spoon, stir in flour well. Pour mixture into prepared tin.
5 Bake cake in moderate oven 50 minutes.
6 Remove cake carefully from oven to work surface; close oven door to maintain correct oven temperature. Using metal spatula, carefully spread warm topping evenly over cake; return cake to oven, bake about 20 minutes or until topping has browned.
7 Stand cake 5 minutes then turn onto wire rack; turn cake top-side up to cool. Cut into slices before serving.

TOPPING Combine ingredients in medium saucepan; using wooden spoon, stir topping mixture over low heat until butter melts and sugar dissolves.

SERVES 12

DATES The fruits of the date palm tree, thought to have originated in North Africa, which have a thick, sticky texture and sweet mild flavour. Sometimes dates are sold already stoned and chopped. They can be eaten fresh or dried on their own, or cooked to release their flavour.

Finely chopping peeled and cored apples

Spreading topping over partially baked cake

TIPS We used Granny Smith apples in this recipe, but any type of apple works just as well.
Standing the apple mixture for 10 minutes allows the bicarbonate of soda to start softening the dates.
Begin preparing the topping while cake is in oven for the first 50 minutes.
The topping can be prepared in a microwave oven. Combine all ingredients in a medium microwave-safe bowl; cook, uncovered, on HIGH (100%) for about 1 minute or until butter melts and sugar dissolves.

biscotti

Meaning 'baked twice', these crisp Italian biscuits are delicious served with coffee or hot chocolate.

coffee & hazelnut biscotti

PREPARATION TIME 35 MINUTES (PLUS SETTING TIME) COOKING TIME 40 MINUTES (PLUS COOLING TIME)

110g CASTER SUGAR
1 EGG, BEATEN LIGHTLY
110g PLAIN FLOUR
½ TEASPOON BAKING POWDER
1 TABLESPOON ESPRESSO-STYLE INSTANT COFFEE
150g HAZELNUTS, TOASTED, CHOPPED COARSELY
100g DARK CHOCOLATE, MELTED

1 Whisk sugar and egg together in medium bowl; stir in flour, baking powder and coffee. Stir in nuts; mix to a sticky dough. Using floured hands, roll into a 20cm (8in) log. Place on greased baking tray.
2 Bake, uncovered, in moderate oven 25 minutes or until lightly browned and firm; cool on tray.
3 Using a serrated knife, cut log, diagonally, into 1cm (½in) slices. Place slices on ungreased baking tray.
4 Bake, uncovered, in moderately low oven about 15 minutes or until dry and crisp, turning halfway through cooking; cool on wire racks.
5 Spread chocolate over one cut side of each biscotti. Allow to set at room temperature.

MAKES 20

choc-almond biscotti

PREPARATION TIME 25 MINUTES (PLUS CHILLING TIME) COOKING TIME 45 MINUTES (PLUS COOLING TIME)

60g BUTTER
220g CASTER SUGAR
1 TEASPOON VANILLA ESSENCE
3 EGGS
335g PLAIN FLOUR
1 TEASPOON BAKING POWDER
½ TEASPOON BICARBONATE OF SODA
240g ALMOND KERNELS, CHOPPED COARSELY
25g COCOA POWDER
35g PLAIN FLOUR, EXTRA

1 Beat butter, sugar and essence in medium bowl until just combined. Add eggs, one at a time, beating until combined between additions. Stir in flour, baking powder, soda and nuts. Cover; refrigerate 1 hour.
2 Halve dough. Knead cocoa into one half of dough; shape into a 30cm (12in) log. Knead extra flour into remaining dough; shape into a 30cm (12in) log. Gently twist cocoa log and plain log together; place on greased baking tray. Bake, uncovered, in moderate oven about 45 minutes or until firm; cool on tray.
3 Using serrated knife cut log, diagonally, into 1cm (½in) slices. Place slices on ungreased baking trays.
4 Bake, uncovered, in moderately low oven about 15 minutes or until dry and crisp, turning halfway through cooking; cool on wire racks.

MAKES 25

lemon & pistachio biscotti

PREPARATION TIME 20 MINUTES (PLUS CHILLING TIME) COOKING TIME 40 MINUTES (PLUS COOLING TIME)

60g BUTTER, CHOPPED COARSELY
220g CASTER SUGAR
1 TEASPOON VANILLA ESSENCE
1 TABLESPOON LEMON RIND
4 EGGS
335g PLAIN FLOUR
1 TEASPOON BAKING POWDER
½ TEASPOON BICARBONATE OF SODA
150g PISTACHIOS, CHOPPED COARSELY
2 TABLESPOONS CASTER SUGAR, EXTRA

1 Beat butter, sugar, essence and rind in medium bowl until just combined. Add three of the eggs, one at a time, beating until combined between additions. Stir in flour, baking powder, soda and nuts. Cover; refrigerate 1 hour.
2 Knead dough on lightly floured surface until smooth but still sticky. Halve dough; shape each half into a 30cm (12in) log. Place each log on greased baking tray. Combine remaining egg with 1 tablespoon water in small bowl. Brush egg mixture over logs; sprinkle thickly with extra sugar.
3 Bake, uncovered, in moderate oven about 20 minutes or until firm; cool on trays.
4 Using serrated knife, cut logs, diagonally, into 1cm (½in) slices. Place slices on ungreased baking trays.
5 Bake, uncovered, in moderately low oven about 15 minutes or until dry and crisp, turning halfway through cooking; cool on wire racks.

MAKES 60

aniseed biscotti

PREPARATION TIME 40 MINUTES (PLUS REFRIGERATION TIME) COOKING TIME 1 HOUR (PLUS COOLING TIME)

125g UNSALTED BUTTER
165g CASTER SUGAR
3 EGGS
2 TABLESPOONS BRANDY
1 TABLESPOON GRATED LEMON RIND
225g PLAIN FLOUR
110g SELF-RAISING FLOUR
½ TEASPOON SALT
125g BLANCHED ALMONDS, TOASTED, CHOPPED COARSELY
1 TABLESPOON GROUND ANISEED

1 Cream butter and sugar in large bowl; add eggs, one at a time, beating well after each addition. Add brandy and rind; mix well. Stir flours and salt into butter mixture.
2 Stir nuts and aniseed into dough; refrigerate, covered, 1 hour.
3 Halve dough; shape each half into a 30cm (12in) log. Place on greased baking tray.
4 Bake, uncovered, in moderate oven 20 minutes or until lightly golden brown; cool on trays.
5 Using serrated knife, cut logs diagonally into 1cm (½in) slices. Place slices on ungreased baking trays.
6 Bake, uncovered, in moderate oven about 25 minutes or until dry and crisp, turning halfway through cooking; cool on wire racks.

MAKES 40

STORAGE All these biscotti recipes can be stored in airtight container for 2 weeks.

christmas & celebration cakes

brandied date cake

The addition of the cream cheese gives this luscious cake an especially moist, rich quality.

PREPARATION TIME 25 MINUTES BAKING TIME 1 HOUR 30 MINUTES

90g BUTTER, SOFTENED
125g CREAM CHEESE, SOFTENED
250g FIRMLY PACKED BROWN SUGAR
3 EGGS
75g PLAIN FLOUR
75g SELF-RAISING FLOUR
60ml BRANDY
380g COARSELY CHOPPED STONED DRIED DATES
85g CANDIED MIXED PEEL
1 TABLESPOON BRANDY, EXTRA

1 Position oven shelves; preheat oven to low. Line base and side of deep 20cm (20in) round cake tin with three thicknesses baking parchment, bringing paper 5cm (2in) above edge of tin.
2 Beat butter, cheese, sugar, eggs, flours and brandy in large bowl on low speed with electric mixer until ingredients are combined. Beat on medium speed until mixture is smooth and changed in colour.
3 Using wooden spoon, mix in dates and peel. Spoon mixture into prepared tin, level surface of cake mixture with wet metal spatula.
4 Bake cake in low oven about 1½ hours.
5 Brush hot cake with extra brandy. Cover tin tightly with foil; cool cake in tin. When cake is cold, and just before serving, decorate if desired by cutting a star shape out of paper; centre paper star on cake then dust top of cake with sifted icing sugar, carefully remove paper star.

SERVES 22

Beating mixture until changed in colour

Brushing hot cake with brandy

TIPS If both butter and eggs are at room temperature, this will help prevent the mixture from curdling.
■ Use commercially made packaged cream cheese, such as full-fat Philadelphia.
■ Cover cake loosely with foil during baking if it starts to brown. too quickly
■ Give the cake quarter turns several times during baking if browning unevenly.

STORAGE Remove cold cake from tin, wrap cake tightly in cling film to keep airtight, then in foil. Wrapped cake can be kept in a cool dark place for about 2 weeks; however, if the climate is humid, keep the cake in a sealed plastic bag or tightly sealed container in the refrigerator. Cake can be frozen for up to 3 months.

TIPS Cake can also be baked in deep 22cm (9in) round cake tin.
- Rum, sherry or your favourite liqueur can be substituted for the brandy.
- The fruit mixture can be made up to a month before required and stored in a cool, dark place – the refrigerator is ideal.
- You can use dark brown or brown sugar rather than black if you prefer.
- Cover cake loosely with foil during baking if it starts to overbrown. Give the cake several quarter turns during baking to avoid uneven browning.
- Because it is quite soft, this cake is best cut cold, after refrigeration.

This cake is very moist, due to the proportion of fruit to flour, which gives it a similar texture to Christmas pudding. Great as a family dessert with custard or, traditionally, for more special occasions such as weddings and birthday parties.

STORAGE Covered cake in tin will go from oven to room temperature in about 24 hours.

- Remove cake from tin by turning cake upside down onto bench, carefully peeling away lining paper from sides of cake but leaving base lining paper in place.
- Wrap cake tightly in cling film to keep airtight, then in wrap in foil.
- Wrapped cake can be kept in a cool dark place for about 12 months; however, if the climate is humid, it is safest to keep the cake in a sealed plastic bag or tightly sealed container in the refrigerator.
- Cake can be frozen for up to 12 months.

rich fruit cake

PREPARATION TIME 30 MINUTES (PLUS STANDING TIME)
BAKING TIME 4 HOURS

380g RAISINS, CHOPPED COARSELY
500g SULTANAS
110g CURRANTS
250g QUARTERED RED GLACÉ CHERRIES
250g COARSELY CHOPPED STONED PRUNES
115g HONEY
125ml BRANDY
250g BUTTER, SOFTENED
200g FIRMLY PACKED BLACK SUGAR
5 EGGS
185g PLAIN FLOUR
2 TABLESPOONS BRANDY, EXTRA

1 Combine fruit, honey and brandy in large bowl, mix well with one hand, cover; stand overnight.
2 Position oven shelves, preheat oven to low. Line base and sides of deep 19cm (7½in) square cake tin with three thicknesses baking parchment, bringing paper 5cm (2in) above sides of tin.
3 Beat butter and sugar in small bowl with electric mixer until just combined; beat in eggs, one at a time, until just combined between additions. Don't worry if mixture curdles at this point; it will come together later.
4 Add creamed mixture to fruit mixture with flour; mix thoroughly with one hand.
5 Drop dollops of mixture into corners of tin to hold paper in position; spread remaining mixture into tin.
6 Drop cake tin from a height of about 15cm (6in) onto work surface to settle mixture into tin and to break any large air bubbles; level surface of cake mixture with wet metal spatula.
7 Bake cake in low oven about 4 hours.
8 Remove cake from oven, brush with extra brandy. Cover tin tightly with foil; cool cake in tin.

SERVES 48

Using your hand to mix ingredients

STORAGE Pies can be made a week ahead. Store pies in airtight container. Pies can be frozen for up to 2 months

mince pies

No traditional Christmas feast would be complete without a batch of these delicious festive treats. Mincemeat is available in jars or you can make your own.

PREPARATION TIME 30 MINUTES (PLUS REFRIGERATION TIME)
BAKING TIME 20 MINUTES

300g PLAIN FLOUR
2 TABLESPOONS GROUND ALMONDS
180g BUTTER
1 TEASPOON GRATED LEMON RIND
40g ICING SUGAR
1 EGG YOLK
60ml MILK, APPROXIMATELY
500g MINCEMEAT
1 EGG, LIGHTLY BEATEN
ICING SUGAR, FOR DUSTING

MINCEMEAT
1 SMALL APPLE, PEELED, CORED
85g SULTANAS
85g CANDIED MIXED PEEL
2 TABLESPOONS GLACÉ CHERRIES, CHOPPED
75g CURRANTS
65g BLANCHED ALMONDS, CHOPPED
200g FIRMLY PACKED BROWN SUGAR
½ TEASPOON GRATED LEMON RIND
1 TABLESPOON LEMON JUICE
½ TEASPOON GRATED ORANGE RIND
½ TEASPOON GROUND CINNAMON
½ TEASPOON MIXED SPICE
¼ TEASPOON GROUND NUTMEG
40g BUTTER, MELTED
2 TABLESPOONS BRANDY

1 Lightly grease two 12-hole shallow bun tray.s
2 Sift flour into bowl, stir in ground almonds, rub in butter. Stir in rind and sifted icing sugar. Stir in yolk and enough milk to make ingredients cling together. Knead dough on floured surface until smooth, cover; refrigerate 30 minutes.
3 Roll pastry until 3mm (⅛in) thick. Cut out 7.5cm rounds, place in bun tray. Drop tablespoons of mincemeat into each pastry case.
4 Roll scraps of pastry on floured surface, cut out desired shapes. Brush each pastry shape with egg, place egg-side down on top of mincemeat.
5 Bake in moderately hot oven about 20 minutes or until lightly browned. Dust with a little sifted icing sugar before serving.

MINCEMEAT Finely chop apple and half the sultanas; combine in bowl with remaining sultanas and remaining ingredients, mix well. Transfer mixture to sterilised jar. Store in refrigerator for at least 3 days before using. Makes about 500g mincemeat.

MAKES 24

STORAGE Pie can be made a day ahead. Store pie covered, in refrigerator. Not suitable for freezing.

Perhaps the most well known pumpkin recipe comes from the United States, in the form of this delicious pie. You will need to cook about 350g pumpkin for this recipe.

pumpkin pie

PREPARATION TIME 30 MINUTES (PLUS REFRIGERATION TIME
BAKING TIME 1 HOUR 10 MINUTES

150g PLAIN FLOUR
35g SELF-RAISING FLOUR
2 TABLESPOONS CORNFLOUR
2 TABLESPOONS ICING SUGAR
125g BUTTER, CHOPPED
2 TABLESPOONS WATER, APPROXIMATELY

FILLING
2 EGGS
50g FIRMLY PACKED BROWN SUGAR
2 TABLESPOONS MAPLE SYRUP
235g COOKED MASHED PUMPKIN
165ml EVAPORATED MILK
1 TEASPOON GROUND CINNAMON
½ TEASPOON GROUND NUTMEG
PINCH GROUND ALLSPICE

1 Sift flours and sugar into bowl, rub in butter. Add enough water to make ingredients cling together. Press dough into a ball, knead gently on floured surface until smooth; cover, refrigerate 30 minutes.
2 Roll dough on floured surface until large enough to line 23cm (9in) pie plate. Lift pastry into pie plate, ease into side; trim edge. Use scraps of pastry to make a double edge of pastry; trim and decorate edge.
3 Place pie plate on oven tray, line pastry with baking parchment, fill with dried beans or rice. Bake in moderately hot oven 10 minutes. Remove paper and beans; bake further 10 minutes or until lightly browned, cool.
4 Pour filling into cooled pastry case; bake in moderate oven about 50 minutes or until filling is set, cool. Lightly dust with extra sifted icing sugar, if desired.

FILLING Beat eggs, sugar and maple syrup in small bowl with electric mixer until thick. Stir in pumpkin, milk and spices.

SERVES 6 TO 8

greek new year's cake

PREPARATION TIME 25 MINUTES BAKING TIME 1 HOUR 15 MINUTES

VASILOPITA
A traditional Greek New Year's cake, vasilopita is traditionally made with a single coin baked into it, legend having it that the person who is served the slice containing the coin will have good luck in the coming year.

■ Many Greek dishes use ingredients full of contrasting flavours and textures with outstanding sweetness or succulence. The use in this cake of lemons, to add a hint of sharpness, and the pistachios to add some bite into the soft cake, are typically Greek.

125g BUTTER, SOFTENED
1 TEASPOON FINELY GRATED LEMON RIND
275g CASTER SUGAR
3 EGGS
75g SELF-RAISING FLOUR
150g PLAIN FLOUR
¼ TEASPOON BICARBONATE OF SODA
125ml MILK
1 TABLESPOON LEMON JUICE
2 TABLESPOONS PISTACHIOS, CHOPPED FINELY
2 TABLESPOONS WALNUTS, CHOPPED FINELY
2 TABLESPOONS SLIVERED ALMONDS, CHOPPED FINELY
2 TEASPOONS ICING SUGAR

NUT TOPPING
2 TABLESPOONS PISTACHIOS, CHOPPED COARSELY
2 TABLESPOONS WALNUTS, CHOPPED COARSELY
2 TABLESPOONS SLIVERED ALMONDS

1 Position oven shelves; preheat oven to moderate. Line base and side of deep 22cm (9in) round cake tin with baking parchment.
2 Combine butter, rind and sugar in small bowl; beat with electric mixer until light and fluffy. Add eggs, one at a time, beating well between additions. Mixture will curdle at this point but will come together later.
3 Using wooden spoon, stir in sifted dry ingredients and milk, in two batches; stir in juice and nuts.
4 Spoon mixture into prepared tin, level surface of cake mixture with wet metal spatula.
5 Bake cake in moderate oven 30 minutes. Cover cake loosely with foil; bake about 45 minutes.
6 Stand cake in tin 5 minutes then turn onto wire rack; turn top-side up to cool. Dust cake with sifted icing sugar before serving.

NUT TOPPING Combine all ingredients in small bowl.

SERVES 14

Chopping nuts finely

Sprinkling cake mixture with nut topping

TIPS This cake can be baked in a deep 19cm (7½in) square cake tin.
■ Mix and match varieties and quantities of nuts to suit your preference.
■ All nuts can be stored in an airtight container in the freezer; they can be used directly from the freezer.

STORAGE Store cake in an airtight container for up to 2 days. Cake can be frozen for up to 3 months.

special occasion cakes

white chocolate mud cake

PREPARATION TIME 30 MINUTES BAKING TIME 2 HOURS

250g BUTTER, CHOPPED COARSELY
150g WHITE CHOCOLATE, CHOPPED COARSELY
440g CASTER SUGAR
250ml MILK
225g PLAIN FLOUR
75g SELF-RAISING FLOUR
1 TEASPOON VANILLA ESSENCE
2 EGGS, BEATEN LIGHTLY

WHITE CHOCOLATE GANACHE
125ml DOUBLE CREAM
300g WHITE CHOCOLATE, CHOPPED COARSELY

1 Position oven shelves; preheat oven to moderately low. Grease deep 20cm (8in) round cake tin; line base and side with baking parchment.
2 Combine butter, chocolate, sugar and milk in medium saucepan; using wooden spoon, stir over low heat, without boiling, until smooth. Transfer mixture to large bowl; cool 15 minutes.
3 Whisk in flours then essence and egg; pour cake mixture into prepared tin.
4 Bake cake in moderately low oven 1 hour. Cover tin loosely with foil; bake about 1 hour. Discard foil, stand cake in tin 10 minutes then turn onto wire rack; turn top-side up to cool.
5 Place cake on serving plate, cover with white chocolate ganache.

WHITE CHOCOLATE GANACHE Bring cream to a boil in small saucepan; pour over chocolate in small bowl, stir with wooden spoon until chocolate melts. Cover bowl; refrigerate, stirring occasionally, about 30 minutes or until ganache is of a spreadable consistency.

SERVES 12

The white chocolate mud cake has rapidly ascended the ladder to the top of the special-occasion favourite-cake list.

TIPS This cake has a high fat and sugar content, and therefore it can be difficult to determine if it is cooked. The method of testing with a skewer is not accurate; following the baking times provided is the best guide, plus the crust on the finished cake should feel quite thick and sugary.
■ If you require a level cake, don't cool the cake top-side up. Turn it out so that the bottom becomes the top of cooled cake that you cover with ganache.

STORAGE Unfrosted cake will keep for up to 1 week in an airtight container at room temperature. Frosted cake will keep for up to 1 week in an airtight container in the refrigerator. Unfrosted cake can be frozen for up to 3 months.

rich truffle mud cake

6 EGGS
100g FIRMLY PACKED BROWN SUGAR
400g DARK CHOCOLATE, MELTED
250ml DOUBLE CREAM (48% FAT CONTENT)
80ml COINTREAU

This very rich cake is perfect for the grand finale to a dinner party, and should be made a day ahead and served cold. The cake is like a huge truffle in texture; note that no flour is used.

TIPS Melt chocolate in medium heatproof bowl placed over saucepan of hot water. Do not allow water in pan to touch the bowl containing chocolate. You can also stand the heatproof bowl in sink of hot water and stir the chocolate until it melts, or melt the chocolate in a microwave-safe bowl on HIGH (100%) in the microwave oven, pausing to check the chocolate every 20 seconds.
■ Any type of liqueur can be substituted for the citrus-flavoured Cointreau; you don't have to have a citrus flavour at all if you prefer some other taste such as rum or Frangelico, etc.
■ The beauty of this cake is that it is completely finished a day ahead of party time.
■ This cake is delicious served with fresh raspberries and fresh raspberry coulis.

STORAGE Cake will keep for up to 4 days in an airtight container in the refrigerator.

PREPARATION TIME 15 MINUTES (PLUS REFRIGERATION TIME)
BAKING TIME 1 HOUR

1 Position oven shelves; preheat oven to moderate. Grease deep 22cm (9in) round cake tin; line base and side with baking parchment.
2 Beat eggs and sugar in large bowl with electric mixer about 5 minutes or until thick and creamy. With motor operating, gradually beat in barely warm chocolate; beat until combined.
3 Using metal spoon, gently fold in combined cream and liqueur. Pour mixture into prepared tin.
4 Place tin in baking dish; pour enough boiling water into dish to come halfway up side of tin.
5 Bake cake in moderate oven 30 minutes. Cover loosely with foil; bake about 30 minutes. Discard foil; cool cake in tin.
6 Turn cake onto serving plate, cover; refrigerate overnight. Serve dusted with a little sifted cocoa, if desired.

SERVES 12

TIPS This cake is best made a day ahead; keep, refrigerated, in airtight container.

If you can't get hold of caramelised almonds, sprinkle some flaked almonds onto a non-stick baking tray, sprinkle generously with icing sugar and bake in a hot oven for a few minutes until golden brown.

Any coffee-flavoured liqueur, such as Kahlua or Tia Maria, can be used in this recipe.

tiramisu torte

PREPARATION TIME 30 MINUTES COOKING TIME 25 MINUTES (PLUS COOLING TIME)

6 EGGS
220g CASTER SUGAR
75g PLAIN FLOUR
75g SELF-RAISING FLOUR
75g CORNFLOUR
10g INSTANT COFFEE GRANULES
375ml BOILING WATER
180ml MARSALA
60ml COFFEE-FLAVOURED LIQUEUR
300ml WHIPPING CREAM
80g ICING SUGAR
750g MASCARPONE
500g CARAMELISED ALMONDS, CHOPPED COARSELY

1 Preheat oven to moderate (180°C/160°C fan-assisted). Grease two deep 22cm (9in) round cake tins; line bases with baking parchment.

2 Beat eggs in medium bowl with electric mixer about 10 minutes or until thick and creamy. Add caster sugar, 1 tablespoon at a time, beating until sugar is dissolved between additions. Gently fold triple-sifted flours into mixture. Divide mixture evenly between tins; bake about 25 minutes. Turn cakes, top-side up, onto wire racks to cool.

3 Meanwhile, dissolve coffee in the boiling water in small heatproof bowl. Stir in marsala and liqueur; cool.

4 Beat cream and icing sugar in small bowl with electric mixer until soft peaks form; transfer to large bowl. Stir in mascarpone and 125ml of the coffee mixture.

5 Split cooled cakes in half. Centre half of one cake on serving plate; brush with a quarter of the remaining coffee mixture then spread with about 250ml of the cream mixture. Repeat layering until last cake half is covered with cream. Spread remaining cream around side of cake; press almonds all over cake. Refrigerate.

SERVES 12

almond meringue cake

PREPARATION TIME 30 MINUTES BAKING TIME 30 MINUTES

- It is thought that meringue was invented by a Swiss pastry-cook called Gasparinig in 1720. It quickly became fashionable in the French court, and it is rumoured that Marie Antoinette herself used to make it with her own regal hands!
- Buy unblanched almonds for maximum usefulness and blanch, toast or roast as required. Always watch carefully whilst toasting as almonds brown very quickly.
- Use good quality eating chocolate, not cooking chocolate or chocolate compounds unless specified. The best chocolate, available from specialist chocolate or food shops, is called couverture and is expensive, although not always more so, weight for weight, than a good quality chocolate bar.

125g BUTTER, SOFTENED
110g CASTER SUGAR
3 EGGS, SEPARATED
150g SELF-RAISING FLOUR
35g COCOA POWDER
125ml BUTTERMILK
120g SOUR CREAM
150g CASTER SUGAR, EXTRA
2 TABLESPOONS FLAKED ALMONDS
160ml WHIPPING CREAM
1 TABLESPOON ICING SUGAR
150g RASPBERRIES

Carefully turning cakes top-side up to cool

Sprinkling raspberries evenly over cream

1 Position oven shelves; preheat oven to moderate. Grease two deep 22cm (9in) round cake tins; line bases with baking parchment.
2 Beat butter, sugar and egg yolks in medium bowl with electric mixer until light and fluffy. Using wooden spoon, stir in combined sifted flour and cocoa, then combined buttermilk and sour cream.
3 Divide mixture evenly between prepared tins.
4 Beat egg whites in small bowl with electric mixer until soft peaks form; gradually add extra sugar, 1 tablespoon at a time, beating until sugar dissolves between additions. Divide meringue mixture evenly over cake mixture in tins; using metal spatula, spread meringue so cake mixture is completely covered. Sprinkle nuts over the meringue on one of the cakes.
5 Bake cakes in moderate oven 10 minutes. Cover tins loosely with foil; bake about 20 minutes. Discard foil; stand cakes in tins 5 minutes then turn onto wire racks. Quickly and carefully turn cakes top-side up to cool.
6 Beat cream and icing sugar in small bowl with rotary or electric mixer until firm peaks form. Place cake without almonds on serving plate; spread cream over top, sprinkle evenly with raspberries, top with remaining cake.

SERVES 12

The combined textures of the soft cake, crisp meringue, crunchy nuts, rich berries and billows of whipped cream make this dessert-cake manna from heaven. It's best made on the day of serving.

TIPS These cakes are quite fragile. After turning out of the tins, it's best to use two wire racks to turn them top-side up. If possible, use two 22cm (9in) springform tins for baking these cakes: when you release the sides of the tins, there is no need to turn the cakes.

When separating the eggs, take care to avoid any yolk getting into the whites or they will not beat to the correct meringue consistency.

STORAGE Cake will keep for 1 day in an airtight container in the refrigerator.

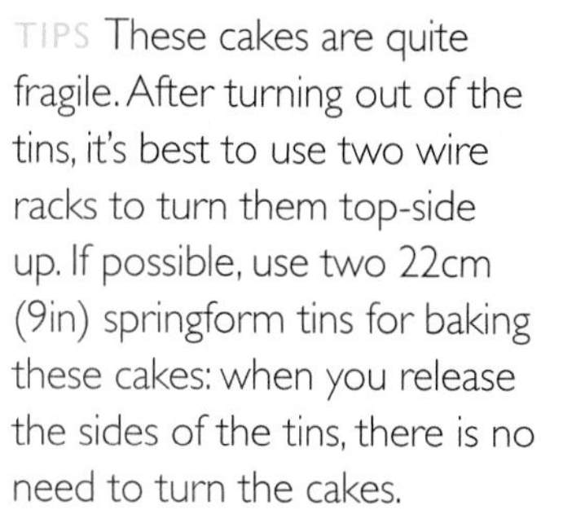

strawberry hazelnut gateau

PREPARATION TIME 1 HOUR
COOKING TIME 35 MINUTES (PLUS COOLING AND REFRIGERATION TIME)

4 EGG WHITES
275g CASTER SUGAR
100g GROUND HAZELNUTS
1 TEASPOON WHITE VINEGAR
½ TEASPOON VANILLA EXTRACT
185g DARK EATING CHOCOLATE, MELTED
20g BUTTER, MELTED
430ml WHIPPING CREAM, WHIPPED
125g STRAWBERRIES, HALVED

1 Preheat oven to moderate (180°C/160°C fan-assisted). Grease two 20cm (8in) springform tins; line base and sides with baking parchment, grease paper, sprinkle with cornflour, shake away excess.
2 Beat egg whites in small bowl with electric mixer until soft peaks form; gradually add sugar, beating until sugar is dissolved between each addition. Fold in ground hazelnuts, vinegar and extract.
3 Spread meringue mixture evenly into tins; bake about 35 minutes or until meringue is crisp. Release sides of tins; cool meringues on base of tins.
4 Combine chocolate and butter in small bowl.
5 Remove meringue layers from bases. Place one layer on plate, flat-side down; spread with half of the chocolate mixture, top with half of the cream and the strawberries.
6 Spread flat side of second meringue layer with remaining chocolate mixture, place on top of strawberry layer, chocolate-side down. Cover top of cake with remaining cream. Refrigerate 3 hours or overnight. Dust with sifted cocoa powder before serving, if desired.

SERVES 8

TIPS Meringue layers can be made 3 days ahead; store in airtight container.
■ Gateau is best assembled the day before; keep, covered, in refrigerator.
■ For a really decedent dessert, completely cover the gateau in whipped cream. This also helps soften the meringue, making it easier to cut.

TIP If you can't get hold of caramelised almonds, sprinkle some whole almonds onto a non-stick baking tray, sprinkle generously with icing sugar and bake in a hot oven for a few minutes until golden brown.

dark chocolate & almond torte

PREPARATION TIME 20 MINUTES COOKING TIME 55 MINUTES (PLUS COOLING AND STANDING TIME)

160g DARK EATING CHOCOLATE, CHOPPED COARSELY
160g BUTTER, CHOPPED
5 EGGS, SEPARATED
165g CASTER SUGAR
120g GROUND ALMONDS
50g TOASTED FLAKED ALMONDS, CHOPPED COARSELY
35g COARSELY GRATED DARK EATING CHOCOLATE
150g CARAMELISED ALMONDS

DARK CHOCOLATE GANACHE
125g DARK EATING CHOCOLATE, CHOPPED COARSELY
80ml WHIPPING CREAM

1 Preheat oven to moderate (180°C/160°C fan-assisted). Grease deep 22cm (9in) round cake tin; line base and side with baking parchment.
2 Stir chopped chocolate and butter in small saucepan over low heat until smooth; cool to room temperature.
3 Beat egg yolks and sugar in small bowl with electric mixer until thick and creamy. Transfer to large bowl; fold in chocolate mixture, ground almonds, flaked almonds and grated chocolate.
4 Beat egg whites in small bowl with electric mixer until soft peaks form; fold into chocolate mixture in two batches. Pour mixture into tin; bake about 45 minutes. Stand cake in tin 15 minutes; turn cake, top-side up, onto wire rack to cool.
5 Meanwhile, stir ingredients for dark chocolate ganache in small saucepan over low heat until smooth.
6 Spread ganache over cake, decorate cake with caramelised almonds; stand 30 minutes before serving.

SERVES 14

citrus polenta cake

A very pretty cake, this is best served warm with lemon mascarpone soon after it is made. Slightly painstaking to make and difficult to slice neatly, but well worth the effort.

165g CASTER SUGAR
310ml WATER
1 MEDIUM UNPEELED ORANGE (240g), SLICED THINLY
1 LARGE UNPEELED LEMON (180g), SLICED THINLY
60ml WATER, EXTRA
125g BUTTER, SOFTENED
1 TABLESPOON FINELY GRATED LEMON RIND
220g CASTER SUGAR, EXTRA
3 EGGS
60g GROUND ALMONDS
75g PLAIN FLOUR
75g SELF-RAISING FLOUR
125g POLENTA
80g SOURED CREAM
60ml LEMON JUICE

LEMON MASCARPONE
250g MASCARPONE CHEESE
2 TEASPOONS FINELY GRATED LEMON RIND
1 TABLESPOON LEMON JUICE
2 TABLESPOONS CASTER SUGAR

Turning orange and lemon slices

Overlapping slices in prepared tin

PREPARATION TIME 20 MINUTES BAKING TIME 1 HOUR 15 MINUTES

1 Position oven shelves; preheat oven to moderate. Grease deep 20cm (8in) round cake tin; line base and side with baking parchment.
2 Combine sugar and the water in large frying pan; using wooden spoon, stir over heat, without boiling, until sugar dissolves. Bring to a boil, reduce heat; simmer, without stirring, uncovered, about 5 minutes or until syrup thickens slightly. Add orange and lemon slices; simmer gently, uncovered, about 7 minutes or until rind is tender, turning slices halfway through cooking time.
3 Remove rind mixture from heat; using tongs, lift alternate orange and lemon slices directly from syrup to cover base and side of prepared tin, slightly overlapping each slice. Reserve syrup.
4 Add the extra water to reserved syrup in pan; bring to a boil. Reduce heat; simmer, uncovered, without stirring, about 5 minutes or until syrup is a light honey colour. Pour hot syrup over orange and lemon slices.
5 Beat butter, rind and extra sugar in small bowl with electric mixer until light and fluffy. Beat in eggs, one at a time, until combined. Mixture will curdle, but will come together later.
6 Transfer mixture to large bowl; using wooden spoon, stir in ground almonds, flours, polenta, soured cream and juice. Carefully spread mixture into prepared pan.
7 Bake cake in moderate oven about 1¼ hours. Stand cake 15 minutes then turn onto serving plate. Serve cake warm with lemon mascarpone.

LEMON MASCARPONE Combine ingredients in small bowl; whisk until smooth.

SERVES 12

TIPS You'll find it best to make the citrus mixture in a large frying pan rather than a saucepan, so that the citrus slices fit in it in a single layer.
■ Polenta is the coarsely ground yellow cornmeal use for making cornmeal muffins and cornbread; it gives this cake a particularly dense texture.

STORAGE Cake will keep for 1 day in an airtight container at room temperature.

STORAGE Ricotta cake is best made a day ahead and can be refrigerated, covered, 3 days.

ricotta cake

PREPARATION TIME 1 HOUR COOKING TIME 1 HOUR (PLUS COOLING TIME)

370g PACKET CHOCOLATE FLAVOUR CAKE MIX
185g RICOTTA CHEESE
55g CASTER SUGAR
2 TABLESPOONS GRAND MARNIER
30g GLACÉ GINGER, CHOPPED FINELY
30g GLACÉ CHERRIES, CHOPPED FINELY
30g DARK CHOCOLATE, CHOPPED FINELY
90g FLAKED ALMONDS, TOASTED

SYRUP
2 TABLESPOONS CASTER SUGAR
80ml WATER
2 TABLESPOONS GRAND MARNIER

ICING
55g CASTER SUGAR
80ml WATER
125g BUTTER
90g DARK CHOCOLATE, MELTED

1 Make up cake mix according to directions on packet; spoon mixture into greased 23cm (9in) round cake tin. Bake in moderate oven about 25 minutes or until cake is cooked when tested; turn onto wire rack to cool.
2 Push cheese through wire sieve into small bowl; beat with electric mixer until smooth and creamy. With motor operating, gradually beat in sugar and Grand Marnier, beating well between additions. Stir in ginger, cherries and chocolate; mix well.
3 Cut cake horizontally into three layers. Place one layer on serving plate; brush with syrup.
4 Spread half of the ricotta mixture over cake. Top with second layer of cake; brush with syrup. Spread with remaining ricotta mixture. Top with remaining layer of cake; brush with syrup.
5 Spread icing over top and side of cake; press nuts around side of cake. Refrigerate until ready to serve; stand at room temperature 10 minutes before serving. Cut into wedges to serve.

SERVES 8

SYRUP Combine sugar, the water and Grand Marnier in small saucepan. Stir over low heat until sugar dissolves; allow to cool.

ICING Place sugar and the water in small saucepan. Stir over low heat until sugar dissolves; bring to a boil. Remove from heat; cool. Beat butter until soft and creamy; gradually beat in cooled syrup, a few drops at a time. Gradually add chocolate to butter mixture; beat until well combined.

STORAGE Zuppa inglese is best made a day ahead and can be refrigerated, covered, 3 days.

CUSTARD FILLING Combine cornflour, custard powder and sugar in large saucepan. Gradually add milk; stir until smooth. Add essence and cream; stir until combined. Stir over low heat until custard boils and thickens; add butter. Simmer, uncovered, 3 minutes, stirring constantly; remove pan from heat. Add yolks; mix well. Transfer custard to medium heatproof bowl; cover surface with plastic wrap. Allow to become cold; beat well.

zuppa inglese

PREPARATION TIME 1 HOUR (PLUS REFRIGERATING TIME)
COOKING TIME 50 MINUTES (PLUS COOLING TIME)

6 EGGS, BEATEN LIGHTLY
275g CASTER SUGAR
150g PLAIN FLOUR
75g CORNFLOUR
1 1/2 TEASPOONS BAKING POWDER
160ml MILK
2 TABLESPOONS RUM
500g STRAWBERRIES
200g BLUEBERRIES
200g RASPBERRIES
2 TEASPOONS ICING SUGAR

CUSTARD FILLING
75g CORNFLOUR
60g CUSTARD POWDER
110g CASTER SUGAR
580ml MILK
2 TEASPOONS VANILLA ESSENCE
300ml WHIPPING CREAM
30g BUTTER
2 EGG YOLKS

1 Beat eggs in medium bowl with electric mixer until thick and creamy. Gradually add sugar; beat until sugar dissolves. Gently fold in flour, cornflour and baking powder. Pour mixture into greased deep 28cm (11in) round cake tin. Bake, uncovered, in moderate oven about 35 minutes or until cake is cooked when tested; turn onto wire rack to cool. Wash and dry cake tin.

2 Split cake, horizontally, into three even layers. Place first layer of cake in clean deep 28cm (11in) round cake tin. Brush cake with combined milk and rum. Spread half of the custard filling evenly over cake. Reserve eight strawberries for decorating top of cake; hull and slice remaining strawberries. Sprinkle half of the sliced strawberries over custard layer. Place second layer of cake on top of strawberries; brush with rum mixture. Spread remaining custard filling evenly over cake; sprinkle with remaining strawberries. Top with third layer of cake; brush with remaining rum mixture. Refrigerate, covered, several hours. [Can be made 2 days ahead to this stage.]

3 Turn cake onto serving plate. Decorate top of cake with reserved strawberries, blueberries and raspberries; dust top of fruit with sifted icing sugar.

SERVES 12

desserts

strawberry pavlova

PREPARATION TIME 25 MINUTES (PLUS COOLING TIME)
COOKING TIME 1 HOUR 30 MINUTES

PAVLOVA This light-as-air dessert was created in 1935 by a chef at the Esplanade Hotel in Perth, Australia, and was named by an employee at the same hotel because, it is said, the confection reminded him of the tutu of the famous Russian ballerina, Anna Pavlova.

4 EGG WHITES
220g CASTER SUGAR
½ TEASPOON VANILLA EXTRACT
¾ TEASPOON WHITE VINEGAR
300ml WHIPPING CREAM, WHIPPED
250g STRAWBERRIES, HALVED

1 Preheat oven to 120°C/100°C fan-assisted. Line oven tray with foil; grease foil, dust with cornflour, shake away excess. Mark 18cm (7in) circle on foil.
2 Beat egg whites in small bowl with electric mixer until soft peaks form; gradually add sugar, beating until sugar dissolves. Add extract and vinegar; beat until combined.
3 Spread meringue into circle on foil, building up at the side to 8cm (3¼in) in height.
4 Smooth side and top of pavlova gently. Using spatula blade, mark decorative grooves around side of pavlova; smooth top again.
5 Bake about 1½ hours. Turn off oven; cool pavlova in oven with door ajar. When pavlova is cold, cut around top edge (the crisp meringue top will fall slightly on top of the marshmallowy centre). Serve pavlova topped with whipped cream and strawberries; dust lightly with sifted icing sugar, if desired.

SERVES 8

STORAGE Store unfilled pavlova in an airtight container for up to 2 days.

Kandle
Sifter
to mix

STORAGE Both pie and crumble can be stored, refrigerated, covered, for up to 1 day.

apple pie

PREPARATION TIME 45 MINUTES (PLUS REFRIGERATION TIME)
COOKING TIME 1 HOUR 10 MINUTES

10 MEDIUM GRANNY SMITH APPLES (1.5kg), PEELED, CORED, SLICED THICKLY
125ml WATER
55g CASTER SUGAR
1 TEASPOON FINELY GRATED LEMON RIND
¼ TEASPOON GROUND CINNAMON
1 TABLESPOON CASTER SUGAR, EXTRA

PASTRY
150g PLAIN FLOUR
75g SELF-RAISING FLOUR
35g CORNFLOUR
30g CUSTARD POWDER
1 TABLESPOON CASTER SUGAR
100g CHILLED BUTTER, CHOPPED
1 EGG, SEPARATED
60ml COLD WATER

1 Make pastry.
2 Place apple with the water in large saucepan; bring to a boil. Reduce heat; simmer, covered, about 10 minutes or until apples soften. Drain; stir in sugar, rind and cinnamon. Cool.
3 Preheat oven to 220°C/200°C fan-assisted. Grease deep 25cm (10in) pie dish.
4 Divide pastry in half. Roll one half between sheets of baking parchment until large enough to line dish. Spoon apple mixture into dish; brush pastry edge with egg white.
5 Roll remaining pastry large enough to cover filling. Press edges together. Brush pastry with egg white; sprinkle with extra sugar. Bake 20 minutes. Reduce oven temperature to 180°C/160°C fan-assisted; bake a further 25 minutes.

PASTRY Process dry ingredients and butter until crumbly. Add egg yolk and the water; process until combined. Knead on floured surface until smooth. Cover; refrigerate 30 minutes.

SERVES 8

apple crumble

PREPARATION TIME 15 MINUTES COOKING TIME 35 MINUTES

5 LARGE APPLES (1kg)
55g CASTER SUGAR
60ml WATER

CRUMBLE
75g SELF-RAISING FLOUR
35g PLAIN FLOUR
110g FIRMLY PACKED BROWN SUGAR
100g CHILLED BUTTER, CHOPPED
1 TEASPOON GROUND CINNAMON

1 Preheat oven to 180°C/160°C fan-assisted. Grease deep 1.5-litre baking dish.
2 Peel, core and quarter apples. Combine apple, sugar and the water in large saucepan; cook over low heat, covered, about 10 minutes. Drain; discard liquid.
3 Meanwhile, make crumble.
4 Place apples in dish; sprinkle with crumble. Bake 25 minutes.

CRUMBLE Blend or process ingredients until combined.

SERVES 4

impossible pie

You'll discover when you make this pie how it got its name: when cooked, the pie magically separates into three perfect layers. Impossible!

75g PLAIN FLOUR
220g CASTER SUGAR
60g DESICCATED COCONUT
4 EGGS
1 TEASPOON VANILLA EXTRACT
125g BUTTER, MELTED
40g FLAKED ALMONDS
500ml MILK

PREPARATION TIME 10 MINUTES COOKING TIME 45 MINUTES

1 Preheat oven to 180°C/160°C fan-assisted. Grease a deep 24cm (9½in) pie dish.
2 Combine sifted flour, sugar, coconut, eggs, extract, butter and half the nuts in large bowl; gradually add milk, stirring, until combined. Pour into dish; bake 35 minutes.
3 Remove pie from oven. Sprinkle remaining nuts over pie; bake 10 minutes. Serve pie with cream or fruit, if desired.

SERVES 8

STORAGE Store impossible pie in refrigerator, covered, for up to 2 days.

STORAGE Store pecan pie in refrigerator, in an airtight container, for up to 3 days.

pecan pie

PREPARATION TIME 25 MINUTES (PLUS REFRIGERATION TIME)
COOKING TIME 1 HOUR

120g PECANS, CHOPPED COARSELY
2 TABLESPOONS CORNFLOUR
220g FIRMLY PACKED BROWN SUGAR
60g BUTTER, MELTED
2 TABLESPOONS CREAM
1 TEASPOON VANILLA EXTRACT
3 EGGS
40g PECANS, EXTRA
2 TABLESPOONS APRICOT JAM, WARMED, SIEVED

PASTRY
185g PLAIN FLOUR
55g ICING SUGAR
125g CHILLED BUTTER, CHOPPED
1 EGG YOLK
1 TEASPOON WATER

1 Make pastry.
2 Grease 24cm (9½in) round loose-based flan tin. Roll pastry between sheets of baking parchment until large enough to line tin. Ease pastry into tin, press into base and side; trim edge. Cover; chill 30 minutes.
3 Preheat oven to 180°C/160°C fan-assisted.
4 Place tin on baking tray. Line pastry case with baking parchment, fill with dried beans or rice. Bake 10 minutes; remove paper and beans carefully from pie shell. Bake about 5 minutes; cool.
5 Reduce oven temperature to 160°C/140°C fan-assisted.
6 Combine chopped nuts and cornflour in medium bowl. Add sugar, butter, cream, extract and eggs; stir until combined. Pour mixture into shell, sprinkle with extra nuts.
7 Bake about 45 minutes. Cool; brush pie with warm jam.

PASTRY Process flour, icing sugar and butter until crumbly. Add egg yolk and water; process until ingredients just come together. Knead on floured surface until smooth. Cover; refrigerate 30 minutes.

SERVES 10

STORAGE Tart can be made a day ahead; keep, covered, in refrigerator.

prune and custard tart

PREPARATION TIME 20 MINUTES (PLUS REFRIGERATION TIME)
COOKING TIME 35 MINUTES (PLUS COOLING TIME)

FILLING
250g STONED PRUNES
2 TABLESPOONS BRANDY
300ml CREAM
3 EGGS
150g CASTER SUGAR
1 TEASPOON VANILLA EXTRACT

PASTRY
185g PLAIN FLOUR
55g ICING SUGAR
30g GROUND ALMONDS
125g CHILLED BUTTER, CHOPPED
1 EGG YOLK
1 TABLESPOON WATER

1 Make pastry; bake tart shell.
2 Reduce oven temperature to low (150°C/130°C fan-assisted).
3 Blend or process prunes and brandy until smooth; spread into cooled tart shell.
4 Bring cream to a boil in small saucepan; remove from heat. Whisk eggs, sugar and extract in small bowl until combined; gradually whisk in hot cream. Pour custard into tart shell; bake, uncovered, about 20 minutes or until custard just sets. Stand 10 minutes; serve tart warm or cold dusted with sifted icing sugar, if desired.

PASTRY Blend or process flour, sugar, ground almonds and butter until mixture is crumbly. Add egg yolk and the water; process until ingredients just come together. Enclose in cling film; refrigerate 30 minutes. Grease 26cm (10in) round loose-based flan tin. Roll pastry between sheets of baking parchment until large enough to line tin. Lift pastry into tin; press into side, trim edge, prick base all over with fork. Cover; refrigerate 20 minutes. Preheat oven to moderately hot (200°C/180°C fan-assisted). Place tin on baking tray; cover pastry with baking parchment, fill with dried beans or rice. Bake, uncovered, 10 minutes. Remove paper and beans carefully from tin; bake about 5 minutes or until tart shell browns lightly. Cool to room temperature.

SERVES 8

■ This delicious tart is such an elegant dessert, and it's a favourite because it is not too rich! Not only is the flavour delicious, but the texture combinations are good too. Use good quality dessert prunes in this recipe and dust the tart with sifted icing sugar just before serving.

TIPS Milk mixture suitable to microwave.
■ Cointreau or boiling water can be substituted for the Grand Marnier.
■ Panettone is a sweet Italian celebration yeast bread; you can also use fruit bread.

STORAGE This recipe is best made on day of serving, but will keep up to 2 days.

panettone & butter pudding

PREPARATION TIME 20 MINUTES (PLUS STANDING TIME)
COOKING TIME 1 HOUR 30 MINUTES (PLUS COOLING TIME)

1kg PANETTONE
90g BUTTER, SOFTENED
750ml MILK
300ml CREAM
110g CASTER SUGAR
5cm PIECE VANILLA POD
2 EGG YOLKS
3 EGGS
80g APRICOT JAM
1 TABLESPOON GRAND MARNIER

1 Preheat oven to moderately low. Grease deep 22cm (9in) ound cake tin; line base and side with baking parchment.
2 Cut panettone in half lengthways, reserve half for another use. Cut in half lengthways again, then crossways into 1.5cm slices. Toast panettone lightly both sides; spread one side with butter while still warm.
3 Slightly overlap slices around sides of prepared tin; layer remaining slices in centre.
4 Combine milk, cream, sugar and split vanilla pod in medium saucepan; stir over heat until mixture comes to a boil. Strain into large jug. Cover; cool 10 minutes.
5 Beat egg yolks and eggs in large bowl; gradually beat in milk mixture. Pour custard over bread in tin.
6 Place cake tin in baking dish; add enough boiling water to dish to come halfway up side of pan.
7 Bake, uncovered, about 1¼ hours or until set. Stand pudding in tin 30 minutes before carefully turning out.
8 Combine jam and liqueur in small bowl; brush evenly over warm pudding. Serve with cream and raspberries, if desired.

SERVES 8

sour cream cheesecake

PREPARATION TIME 30 MINUTES (PLUS REFRIGERATION TIME)
COOKING TIME 50 MINUTES (PLUS COOLING TIME)

- 250g DIGESTIVE BISCUITS
- 150g BUTTER, MELTED
- 250g CREAM CHEESE, SOFTENED
- 250g COTTAGE CHEESE
- 3 EGGS
- 220g CASTER SUGAR
- 2 TABLESPOONS CORNFLOUR
- 125ml MILK
- 240g SOURED CREAM
- 1 TABLESPOON FINELY GRATED LEMON RIND
- 1 TEASPOON LEMON JUICE

1 Preheat oven to moderately low (170°C/150°C fan-assisted).
2 Blend or process biscuits until mixture resembles fine breadcrumbs. Add butter; process until combined. Press biscuit mixture evenly over base and side of 20cm (8in) springform tin, place on baking tray; refrigerate about 30 minutes or until firm.
3 Meanwhile, beat cheeses together until smooth. Beat in eggs, one at a time. Stir in sugar and cornflour then milk, cream, rind and juice; pour into crumb crust.
4 Bake about 50 minutes. Cool in oven with door ajar. Refrigerate overnight.

SERVES 8

TIPS Soufflés must be made just before serving.
■ We used Grand Marnier in this recipe, but you can use any citrus-flavoured liqueur, such as Curacao or Cointreau.

hot passionfruit soufflé with raspberry cream

This is the perfect beginner's 'scared-to-make-a-soufflé', foolproof recipe.

PREPARATION TIME 25 MINUTES COOKING TIME 10 MINUTES

1 TABLESPOON CASTER SUGAR
2 EGGS, SEPARATED
6 PASSIONFRUIT, PEELED AND PULPED
2 TABLESPOONS LEMON JUICE
120g ICING SUGAR
4 EGG WHITES

RASPBERRY CREAM
125g FROZEN RASPBERRIES, THAWED
300ml WHIPPING CREAM
1 TABLESPOON ICING SUGAR
1 TABLESPOON ORANGE-FLAVOURED LIQUEUR

1 Make raspberry cream. Refrigerate until required.
2 Preheat oven to hot (220°C/200°C fan-assisted). Lightly grease four 250ml soufflé dishes, sprinkle inside each one with caster sugar; shake away excess.
3 Combine yolks, passionfruit, juice and half of the sifted icing sugar in large bowl.
4 Beat all the egg whites in small bowl with electric mixer until soft peaks form; add remaining sifted icing sugar and continue beating until firm peaks form. Gently fold a quarter of the whites into passionfruit mixture, then fold in remaining whites.
5 Place dishes on oven tray. Spoon soufflé mixture into prepared dishes; bake about 10 minutes or until puffed and browned.
6 Dust soufflés with a little extra sifted icing sugar, if desired. Serve immediately with raspberry cream.

RASPBERRY CREAM Push thawed raspberries through sieve to remove seeds. Whip cream and icing sugar until soft peaks form, beat in sugar; fold in the raspberry puree and liqueur.

SERVES 4

TIP Golden delicious apples will give you the best results in this recipe.

STORAGE Apple caramel mixture and pastry can be made a day ahead; store separately, covered, in the refrigerator.

tarte tatin

PREPARATION TIME 30 MINUTES (PLUS REFRIGERATION TIME)
COOKING TIME 45 MINUTES (PLUS COOLING TIME)

2 TABLESPOONS ORANGE JUICE
150g CASTER SUGAR
70g BUTTER
3 MEDIUM APPLES (450g), PEELED

PASTRY
150g PLAIN FLOUR
80g CHILLED BUTTER, CHOPPED
1 TABLESPOON CASTER SUGAR
1 TABLESPOON COLD WATER, APPROXIMATELY

PASTRY Blend or process flour, butter and sugar until mixture resembles fine breadcrumbs. Add enough water to make ingredients just cling together. Knead dough on floured surface until smooth. Cover, refrigerate 1 hour.

1 Combine juice, sugar and butter in 23cm (9in) heavy-based ovenproof frying pan; stir over heat, without boiling, until sugar is dissolved. Simmer, stirring occasionally, until mixture becomes a thick, light golden caramel. Remove from heat.
2 Halve apples; cut each half into three wedges, remove cores. Pack apple wedges, rounded-sides down, tightly into pan over caramel, return to heat; simmer, uncovered, about 15 minutes or until most of the liquid is evaporated and caramel is dark golden brown. Remove from heat; cool 1 hour.
3 Meanwhile, make pastry.
4 Preheat oven to moderate (180°C/160°C fan-assisted).
5 Roll pastry into circle a little larger than the frying pan. Lift pastry, without stretching it, on top of apples, tuck inside edge of pan. Bake about 25 minutes or until pastry is golden brown and crisp. Remove tarte from oven, stand 5 minutes.
6 Carefully invert tarte onto plate. Serve warm with cream, if liked.

SERVES 6

STORAGE Pie best made a day ahead; keep, covered, in refrigerator.

The key lime flourishes in Florida, in the United States, where it's used in many dishes. There are many variations of this famous American recipe, but this is our favourite.

key lime pie

150g PLAIN FLOUR
2 TEASPOONS ICING SUGAR
60g BUTTER
2 TEASPOONS LEMON JUICE
1 TABLESPOON WATER, APPROXIMATELY

FILLING
180g SWEETENED CONDENSED MILK
200g RICOTTA CHEESE
3 EGGS, SEPARATED
2 TEASPOONS GRATED LEMON RIND
80ml LIME JUICE

FILLING Blend or process milk, cheese, egg yolks, rind and juice until smooth; transfer to large bowl. Beat egg whites in small bowl until soft peaks form, fold into lime mixture in 2 batches.

PREPARATION TIME 30 MINUTES (PLUIS REFRIGERATION TIME)
COOKING TIME 35 MINUTES (PLUS COOLING TIME)

1 Sift flour and icing sugar into bowl, rub in butter. Stir in lemon juice and enough water to mix to a soft dough. Knead dough gently on floured surface until smooth; cover, refrigerate 30 minutes.
2 Roll dough between sheets of baking parchment until large enough to fit 23cm (9in) pie plate. Lift pastry into pie plate, ease into side of plate; trim edge.
3 Place pie plate on baking tray, line pastry with baking parchment, fill with dried beans or rice. Bake in moderately hot oven 10 minutes. Remove paper and beans; bake further 7 minutes or until lightly browned. Cool.
4 Pour filling into pastry case; bake in moderate oven about 25 minutes or until filling is set. Cool.
5 Refrigerate pie until well chilled; dust with sifted icing sugar just before serving.

SERVES 6–8

glossary

ALMONDS
flaked paper-thin slices.
ground nuts are powdered to a flour-like texture, for use in baking or as a thickening agent.
slivered small lengthways-cut pieces.

BAKING POWDER raising agent consisting mainly of two parts cream of tartar to one part bicarbonate of soda.

BICARBONATE OF SODA also known as baking soda.

BRANDY short for brandywine, the translation of the Dutch 'brandwijn', burnt wine. A general term for a liqueur distilled from wine grapes (usually white), it is used as the basis for many sweet-to-dry spirits made with fruits. Cognac and Armagnac are two of the finest aged brandies.

BRIOCHE French in origin; a rich, yeast-leavened, cake-like bread made with butter and eggs. Most common form is the brioche à tête, a round fluted roll topped with a much smaller ball of dough. Available from cake or specialty bread shops.

BUTTER use salted or unsalted butter.

BUTTERMILK sold alongside fresh milk products in supermarkets. A good lower-fat substitute for dairy products such as cream or sour cream; good in baking and in salad dressings.

CHOCOLATE
chocolate chips available in milk, white and dark chocolate. These hold their shape in baking and are ideal as a cake decoration.
dark cooking we used premium-quality dark cooking chocolate rather than compound.
dark eating made of cocoa liquor, cocoa butter and sugar.
milk eating most popular eating chocolate, mild and very sweet; similar in make-up to dark with the difference being the addition of milk solids.
white eating contains no cocoa solids but derives its sweet flavour from cocoa butter. Very sensitive to heat.

CINNAMON dried inner bark of the shoots of the cinnamon tree; available in stick or ground form.

COCOA POWDER unsweetened, dried, roasted ground cocoa beans.

COCONUT
desiccated unsweetened, concentrated, dried shredded coconut.
flaked dried, flaked coconut flesh.
shredded thin strips of dried coconut flesh.

COFFEE-FLAVOURED LIQUEUR an alcoholic syrup distilled from wine or brandy and flavoured with coffee. Use Tia Maria, Kahlua or any other coffee-flavoured liqueur.

COLOURINGS many types are available from cake decorating suppliers, craft shops and supermarkets; all are concentrated. Use a minute amount of any type of colouring first to determine its strength.
liquid the strength varies depending on the quality; useful for colouring most types of icings where pastel colours are needed. Large amounts of liquid colourings will dilute or break down most icings.
powdered these are edible and are used when primary colours or black are needed.
concentrated pastes these are a little more expensive but are the easiest to use; are suitable for both pastel and stronger colours.

CORNFLOUR also known as cornstarch; used as a thickening agent in cooking.

CREAM
sour (minimum fat content 35%) a thick, commercially cultured soured cream.
thick (minimum fat content 48%) a rich, pure cream not suitable for whipping.
whipping (minimum fat content 35%) a whipping cream containing a thickener.

CURRANTS tiny, almost-black raisins, named after a grape variety originating in Corinth, Greece.

CUSTARD POWDER packaged powdered mixture of starch (wheat or corn), artificial flavouring and colouring. Sometimes sold as vanilla pudding mixture.

DATES fruits of the date palm tree, thought to have originated in North Africa, which have a thick, sticky texture and sweet mild flavour. Sometimes sold already stoned and chopped; can be eaten fresh or dried on their own, or cooked to release their flavour.

ESSENCE also known as extract; a flavouring extracted from various plants by distillation.

FLOUR

plain an all-purpose flour, made from wheat.

self-raising all-purpose flour sifted with baking powder in the proportion of 150g flour to 2 teaspoons baking powder.

wholemeal also known as all-purpose wholemeal flour; has no baking powder added.

GELATINE we use dried (powdered) gelatine in the recipes in this book; it's also available in sheet form known as leaf gelatine. Three teaspoons of dried gelatine (8g or one sachet) is roughly equivalent to four gelatine leaves. The two types are interchangable, but leaf gelatine gives a much clearer mixture than dried gelatine; it's perfect in dishes where appearance really counts.

GLACÉ CHERRIES also known as candied cherries; cherries cooked in heavy sugar syrup then dried.

GOLDEN SYRUP a by-product of refined sugarcane; pure maple syrup or honey can be substituted.

HAZELNUTS also known as filberts; plump, grape-sized, rich, sweet nut having a brown inedible skin that is removed by rubbing heated nuts together vigorously in a tea towel.

ground hazelnuts the nut is roasted then powdered to a flour-like texture for use in baking.

JAM also known as preserves or conserve.

MACADAMIA native to Australia, a rich and buttery nut; store in the refrigerator because of its high oil content.

MAPLE-FLAVOURED SYRUP made from sugar cane rather than maple-tree sap; used in cooking or as a topping but cannot be considered an exact substitute for pure maple syrup.

MARSALA a sweet fortified wine originally from Sicily.

MASCARPONE a fresh, unripened, thick, triple-cream cheese with a delicately sweet, slightly acidic flavour.

MINCEMEAT a mixture of dried fruits, peel, rind, sugar, alcohol and spices. When cooked, the mixture forms a rich, fruity spread; commonly used as a filling in fruit mince pies.

MIXED FRUIT also known as mixed dried fruit; commonly a combination of sultanas, raisins, currants, mixed peel and cherries. mixed peel also known as candied citrus peel.

MIXED PEEL candied citrus peel.

MIXED SPICE a classic mixture generally containing caraway, allspice, coriander, cumin, nutmeg and ginger, although cinnamon and other spices can be added.

NUTMEG a strong and very pungent spice ground from the dried nut of an evergreen tree native to Indonesia. Usually found ground, but the flavour is more intense from a whole nut, available from spice shops, so it's best to grate your own.

PECAN native to the United States and now grown locally; golden-brown, buttery and rich in flavour.

POLENTA a flour-like cereal made of ground corn (maize); similar to cornmeal but finer and paler.

RICOTTA sweet, moist, fresh curd cheese having a low fat content.

RIND also known as zest; the outer layer of all citrus fruits.

SUGAR we used coarse, granulated table sugar, also known as crystal sugar, unless otherwise specified.

black less refined than brown sugar and containing more molasses; mostly used in making Christmas cakes, this is available from health food stores.

brown a soft, fine granulated sugar containing molasses to give its characteristic colour.

caster also known as superfine or finely granulated table sugar.

demerara small-grained, golden-coloured crystal sugar.

icing sugar also known as confectioners' sugar or powdered sugar; crushed granulated sugar

SULTANAS also known as golden raisins; dried, seedless, white grapes.

TREACLE thick, dark syrup not unlike molasses; a by-product of refined sugar.

VANILLA ESSENCE distilled from the seeds of the vanilla pod; imitation vanilla extract is not a satisfactory substitute.

VEGETABLE OIL any of a number of oils sourced from plants rather than animal fats.

index

conversion charts

WARNING This book contains recipes for dishes made with raw or lightly cooked eggs. These should be avoided by vulnerable people such as pregnant and nursing mothers, invalids, the elderly, babies and young children.

MEASURES

- The spoon measurements used in this book are metric: one metric tablespoon holds 20ml; one metric teaspoon holds 5ml.
- All spoon measurements are level.
- The most accurate way of measuring dry ingredients is to weigh them.
- When measuring liquids, use a clear glass or plastic jug with metric markings.
- We use large eggs with an average weight of 60g.

DRY MEASURES

metric	imperial
15g	1/2oz
30g	1oz
60g	2oz
90g	3oz
125g	4oz (1/4lb)
155g	5oz
185g	6oz
220g	7oz
250g	8oz (1/2lb)
280g	9oz
315g	10oz
345g	11oz
375g	12oz (3/4lb)
410g	13oz
440g	14oz
470g	15oz
500g	16oz (1lb)
750g	24oz (1 1/2lb)
1kg	32oz (2lb)

LIQUID MEASURES

metric	imperial
30ml	1 fl oz
60ml	2 fl oz
100ml	3 fl oz
125ml	4 fl oz
150ml	5 fl oz (1/4 pint/1 gill)
190ml	6 fl oz
250ml	8 fl oz
300ml	10 fl oz (1/2 pt)
500ml	16 fl oz
600ml	20 fl oz (1 pint)
1000ml (1 litre)	1 3/4 pints

LENGTH MEASURES

metric	imperial
3mm	1/8in
6mm	1/4in
1cm	1/2in
2cm	3/4in
2.5cm	1in
5cm	2in
6cm	2 1/2in
8cm	3in
10cm	4in
13cm	5in
15cm	6in
18cm	7in
20cm	8in
23cm	9in
25cm	10in
28cm	11in
30cm	12in (1ft)

OVEN TEMPERATURES

These oven temperatures are only a guide for conventional ovens. For fan-assisted ovens, check the manufacturer's manual.

	°C (Celcius)	°F (Fahrenheit)	gas mark
Very low	120	250	1/2
Low	150	275-300	1-2
Moderately low	170	325	3
Moderate	180	350-375	4-5
Moderately hot	200	400	6
Hot	220	425-450	7-8
Very hot	240	475	9